SCOTTISH CASTLES

Martin Horan

Chambers

CHAMBERS
An imprint of Larousse plc
43–45 Annandale Street
Edinburgh EH7 4AZ

First published by Chambers 1994

A CIP catalogue record for this book is available from
the British Library

ISBN 0550 20073 8

Illustrations by Julie Horan
© Julie Horan

Typeset by Pillans & Wilson Ltd
Fdinburgh, Glasgow, London and Manchester
Printed in Singapore by
Singapore National Printers Ltd

Introduction

Castles and fortifications have been built in Scotland from the earliest times—whether by the natives or the first settlers. In AD80 the Roman governor Julius Agricola built several forts north of the Clyde. Prior to that time the Strathclyde Britons had some kind of great fortress at Alcluyd, now Dumbarton. The brochs in the north attest to fortresses being built during the Iron Age in (what was much later to be called) Scotland.

Prior to the Norman Conquest most fortifications—certainly those that can be loosely termed 'castles'—were made of earth and timber. Though there are no Norman castles in Scotland the idea of building fortified stone residences, especially with keeps, came via the Normans.

Scotland being one of the farthest edges of European influence, the development of Scottish castles into a more apt design for defensive purposes was slower than in those areas nearer to the centre of European civilization. The same applied in aesthetic design. As wealth and cultural influence were late arrivals to Scotland, its nobles had neither the wealth nor the inclination to erect the kind of Gothic and Renaissance wonders we see in Europe.

This does not mean that Scotland has not produced wonders of her own in castle architecture. Her cultural isolation brought about a development of peculiarly Scottish fortified houses. Though these are built for the most part on two plans (L and Z) there was still much room for individual interpretation—in size as much as in design. Later additions and subtractions have added to the variety of overall design.

As lawlessness continued in Scotland (as well as in northern England and Ireland) for several generations after the peaceful Tudor reign in southern England, these strong fortified houses were required for the troubled times, while the government too required garrisons for the militia.

The Act of Union (1707) meant closer ties with

England and, besides more wealth for the Scottish nobles, a wider exposure to English architectural developments. The castles built at this time were more a statement of wealth and cultural refinement than defences; some of the finest British 'pretend castles' were built in Scotland. In spite of English influences a uniquely Scottish design arose out of them — Scottish Baronial.

The castles I have chosen for this book range from Gothic times up to Victorian, selected also with their accessibility to the reader in mind. Fortunately, Scotland is not a large country and even the Highlands and outermost islands are now reachable by both visitors and residents. Thankfully, the most accessible castles are those of the most historical and architectural interest!

Though such a book is almost inevitably a personal selection, I have endeavoured to cover every region in Scotland and every type of Scottish castle, ruin or otherwise, whether clan seat, nobleman's residence or military fortress, to give a sense of the enormous richness and variety of the Scottish castle tradition.

List of Scottish Castles

Aberdour Castle
Balmoral Castle
Balvenie Castle
Blackness Castle
Blair Castle
Borthwick Castle
Bothwell Castle
Braemar Castle
Brodick Castle
Brodie Castle
Caerlaverock Castle
Castle Campbell
Castle Fraser
Cawdor Castle
Claypotts Castle
Corgarff Castle
Craigievar Castle
Craigmillar Castle
Crathes Castle
Crichton Castle
Culzean Castle
Dirleton Castle
Doune Castle
Drum Castle
Drumlanrig Castle
Duart Castle
Duffus Castle

Dunnottar Castle
Dunvegan Castle
Edinburgh Castle
Edzell Castle
Eilean Donan Castle
Elcho Castle
Falkland Palace
Glamis Castle
Hermitage Castle
Palace of
   Holyroodhouse
Huntingtower Castle
Huntly Castle
Inveraray Castle
Kellie Castle
Kildrummy Castle
Linlithgow Palace
Loch Leven Castle
Noltland Castle
Rothesay Castle
St Andrews Castle
Stirling Castle
Tantallon Castle
Threave Castle
Tolquhon Castle
Urquhart Castle

Aberdour Castle

Aberdour, Fife

Historic Scotland, open to the public.

Aberdour Castle, by the village of the same name, stands on a ridge of ground overlooking the Forth estuary. It once consisted of three sections, the oldest having been a keep on the north-west corner which stood on the highest ground. This collapsed in 1844. The two other sections have been in ruins since the 18th century. Since then the castle has been quarried frequently to provide stone for other buildings. It is believed that it was partially destroyed in 1688 and/or burnt down in 1715 when occupied by troops. There is no firm evidence to support either theory.

The castle was first built in the 14th century, several years after the site had been granted by Robert Bruce to his close friend and nephew Thomas Randolph, Earl of Moray. This post was the original tower which was modified in the following century. This was to create greater accommodation space and entailed rebuilding the top storey. It also included erecting a new square-plan staircase tower on the south-east corner adjacent to the part of the wall containing the original spiral staircase.

Unlike most great towers, the entrance was at ground — and not first — floor level.

The first addition was probably the work of the Regent Morton, who was executed in 1581. He took the castle from the powerful Douglases into whose hands it had passed some two hundred years prior. Morton's descendants abandoned the ruins in 1725. The castle had been burnt during the previous century and thereafter allowed to deteriorate. An ornamental garden was erected in the courtyard to the south, however, and was maintained.

Though built on the lines of an ancient keep, some reckon it was executed in a manner that threw off the traditional restraints in keep and courtyard erection. Through this approach, well-lit and expanded accommodation was achieved.

1

Ruins of a chapel stand on the south side of the garden. Part of the chapel dates from the Norman period when it belonged to the prior of St Colme's inch.

The original castle started as a rhombodial great tower, though little of that remains today except for some walling. All that survives intact is the extreme eastern range which consists of an oblong block. It has two small northward projections and a square wing to the south, possibly 17th century. This rebuilt part of the castle was at various times used as a barrack, school, masonic hall and a dwelling till 1924. It was then given to the Scottish Development Department Agency, predecessor of Historic Scotland.

There is a low square tower in the re-entrant angle, now housing the entrance and stairway. Originally, it may have been a larger tower forming part of the courtyard.

On the pediment of the upper floor pillastered window are the initials of the 7th earl (d. 1648). They also adorn a sundial on the corner of the south wing, entwined with those of his wife.

The castle entrance is a 17th-century Renaissance gateway, guarded by gunlaps.

Another feature of interest to the visitor is an ambitious restoration of the terraced garden by Historic Scotland.

Balmoral Castle

Deeside, Grampian

Privately owned, open to the public.

Balmoral is the private residence of HM the Queen in Crathie parish on the southern bank of the Dee. Used by the royal family as a summer retreat, it stands on a level terrace against a spectacular backdrop of 3000 feet high wooded hills. It is 926 feet above sea level and commands magnificent views of Deeside.

Prince Albert bought the Balmoral estate in 1852, for £31000, from the Earl of Fife. The present white granite building was completed in 1855 by William Smith of Aberdeen, at a cost of £100000. It is in Scottish baronial style and its main feature is the 100 feet high east tower.

There was an early medieval manor on the site, known as Kindrochit. It was a favourite hunting lodge of Robert II. In 1390 a tower was erected there. The estate had belonged to the Gordons of Huntly from the 15th century till it passed to the Farquharsons of Inverey in 1662. (There is a local legend that when they set off to battle each of the Farquharsons put a stone on a cairn; on their return each man removed a stone. The remaining stones showed the number of casualties.) They held on to it till 1798. Bored by the bad weather at their former holiday home at Ardverikie, on Loch Laggan, the royal family were on the lookout for such a place.

Believed to be the largest castle in Scotland, it has had many critics. Disraeli loathed it. Harcourt called it 'a hole'; Lady Dalhousie said: 'I never saw anything more uncomfortable and that I coveted less.' Prince Leopold's 'intense aversion' to Balmoral made him refuse to go there at all, much to his mother, Queen Victoria's, extreme anger.

Balvenie Castle

Argyll, Strathclyde

Historic Scotland, ruin, open to the public.

Balvenie Castle stands on a rock in the valley of the River Fiddich, half a mile north of Dufftown. Built c. 1296, it is one of the oldest examples of a stone castle in north-east Scotland. It must have been an impressive fortress in its day because, as a ruin, it still gives the impression of impregnability.

It consists of a strong high wall of *enceinte* surrounding a quadrangle court measuring 150 by 130 feet. It was protected by a wide ditch, 30 to 40 feet from the wall. Part of it still remains on the south-west and north-west sides.

Balvenie, like many other Scottish castles, has been renovated and added to over the years. The north-east side was altered from the original plan, probably during the 16th century. The living rooms of the *L*-shaped, four-storey castle were originally at the north-west and south-east sides of the courtyard. They were made of wood and stone and are thought to have been burnt down at some stage.

Two towers face into the courtyard — at the west and north corners — and there was probably one

at the east where the 16th-century round tower now stands. The largest one, corbelled square over the third storey to provide a narrow gabled watchroom, once contained the main stair.

From the outside, the two building periods are quite visible. In the 16th century the northern half of the main building, a fortress, was demolished. John Stewart, the 4th Earl of Atholl, had it rebuilt as a stately family residence. However, split and blistered freestone shows that part had been destroyed by fire.

Entry into the castle is through a vaulted arch, or pend, with splayed-ended gun loops at either side. It has a double-leafed yett, the only one of its kind in Scotland. A guardroom lies to the left. Above the entrance are the royal arms of Scotland and the arms of Stewart of Atholl, along with the motto *Furth fortuin and fil thi fatris*. In fact, the entrances from the courtyard to the two stair towers are all intricately carved and moulded.

Balvenie witnessed much fighting during the 17th century. Montrose billeted his men there in 1644, after the Battle of Fyvie. Five years later a band of royalists were defeated there; 80 men died in battle.

Balvenie, which had been in the hands of the Stewart Earls of Atholl until the 17th century, came under different ownership several times. It was bought in 1614 by one of the Innes family. They sold it in 1658 to a Colonel Sutherland of Kinminity. The next owner was Alexander Duff of Branco who took possession in 1687. It remained with the Duffs throughout the 1700s.

In 1928 the trustees handed over the castle to the Scottish Development Department and it is now owned by Historic Scotland.

Blackness Castle

West Lothian, Lothian

Historic Scotland, open to the public.

Blackness Castle once guarded the village of the same name, when a sea port of Linlithgow, from its rocky headland on the River Forth. It is 3.5 miles from Bo'ness and roughly 15.5 miles west of Edinburgh. It was once a very important fortress by virtue of this strategic position.

Originally, when built in the 15th century, it was an oblong keep. Now this is the central part of the castle, the 'main mast' tower, probably so-called as the overall plan is very much like that of a ship. The tower stands inside the 'ship shape' courtyard—of mainly 16th-century construction—which has another tower at one end, and a triangular tower-like bastion at the 'bow' end of the courtyard. The latter has a pit prison beneath the ground floor. Around 1667, a turnpike was added at the north-east angle for the tower itself to be used as a prison.

Around the castle is a 16th-century barmkin wall, widened internally in the 17th century for the construction of a cannon platform.

It has had various owners and occupiers: the Douglases, the Crichtons, Mary Queen of Scots, the French in 1548, the Regent, the Stewarts, the Livingstons, and the English when Monk captured it in 1654. Because of the damage the English inflicted on Blackness Castle, Charles II had to have it repaired.

Over a hundred years prior to that, work began under Sir James Hamilton of Finnart, which was to include a thickening of the exposed walls with ample provision for defending guns. These alterations transformed the castle into one of the most effective artillery fortifications in 16th-century Scotland.

The main doorway is an iron yett, the passage of which leads to the kitchen and to the vaulted gun chambers on the lower floor as well as to a large hall on the second floor. Last century it was restored by the government to its 17th-century outline.

This austere-looking castle often served as a prison and it looks like one, with its featureless main walls and lack of windows, the main ones being grilled. Cardinal Beaton was imprisoned there in 1543, as was the Earl of Angus the following year. In 1453, James Crichton, furious at his father for — as he saw it — throwing away his inheritance, imprisoned him there. Indeed, one of the castle's horrors is its pit prison. This miserable, dank dungeon contains a drain which was cleansed by the tide.

It became an unimportant garrison after the Act of Union (1707) and then, in 1870, it was converted into an arsenal. It ceased to be used by the military after World War I and was taken over by the government. Nearly all of the buildings erected after 1870 were demolished — except for the barracks, the pier and its drawbridge. In 1930–3, the upper parts of the tower were rebuilt to resemble the original appearance.

Blair Castle

Blair Atholl, Perth and Kinross

Privately owned, open to the public.

The great white-harled baronial Blair Castle can be seen from a stretch of the A9 between the east of Calvine and the north of Pitlochry. It is perched on the steep slopes behind Blair Atholl village.

The castle has a long history and has been the seat of the Dukes of Atholl — originally the Earls of Strathbogie — from Celtic times. The last earl had his title revoked for opposing Robert Bruce. His descendants have held the lands since 1457.

Possibly only the foundations of the original tower remain. If so, they are the oldest part. The parapeted flat-roofed and crenellated tower to the right of the entrance may be 15th century. It is claimed that the hall range was built in 1530 by the Stewart earl. The vaulted rooms beneath it were built at the same time.

The castle was captured and 'destroyed by powder' by the Cromwellian commander Daniel. It must have been restored by 1689 as Claverhouse used it as a garrison. Soon after the 2nd marquis was made a duke, he carried out more renovations. His son, the 2nd duke, commissioned schemes to palladianize the castle and apparently began to extend it.

More building work was required after a younger brother of the 2nd duke laid seige to it

during the 1745 rising. This made Blair Atholl the last castle in the British Isles ever to be beseiged. Embarrassed by these events, the duke later docked the castle of its parapets, turrets and two top storeys. He had its facade remodelled in plain vernacular style by James Winter, turning it into a country house. He even renamed it Atholl House. When Queen Victoria arrived at Blair in 1844 she described it as a 'large plain white building'. Twenty-five years later — by which time the Georgian style had waned — the 7th duke engaged John and David Bryce to restore it to the full baronial style. Turrets, bartisans and crow-steps reappeared, and the present Fyvie-inspired front entrance and a ballroom to the south were added. The castle is now an excellent and dignified monument to Scottish baronialism.

The interior is still decorated in luxurious 18th-century style. It is famed for its superb rococo ceiling and walls, created by the great plasterer Thomas Clayton, and for the work of the English carpenter Abraham Swan. The rooms are furnished with fine examples of the period, including outstanding pieces of Chippendale and Sheraton. A collection of Sèvres porcelain is on display as are paintings by well-known artists such as Lely and Raeburn. The latter's famous painting of Neil Gow, the legendary fiddler, is on view.

Various rooms house collections of armour and weapons, illustrating different periods and military campaigns. The duke retains the only private army in Britain, the Atholl Highlanders.

Borthwick Castle

Midlothian, Lothian

Tower house, privately owned, not open to the public.

There is something proud and defiant in the look of Borthwick Castle. Hardly surprising, as it is the highest tower house in Scotland as well as one of the best-preserved and most impressive of our medieval buildings.

Standing just to the east of the hamlet of Middleton, roughly 13 miles from Edinburgh, this double tower of dressed ashlar rises to a height of 110 feet. The fact that the few windows it does have are small and thin makes the sheer plain walls appear all the more impregnable — as does the fact that they are dressed ashlar. Borthwick does not have any gun loops as the walls were considered to be sufficient defence. The machicolated parapets, behind which stand gables on each tower, must have been the safest place in medieval Scotland for a soldier to be during battle!

One can understand why it was selected during World War II to shelter many of Scotland's art treasures from possible attacks from Hitler's *Luftwaffe*.

The castle was bombarded by Cromwell in 1650, however, during the war between Scotland and England. When the 9th Lord Borthwick refused to surrender after a written threat from Cromwell, the latter's cannon opened fire on the fortress walls. Though little damage was done, Borthwick surrendered. The results of the bombardment can still be seen on a few parts of the battlements and on some parts of the east main wall. They slightly mar the otherwise neat appearance of the castle's masonry. As the walls are so thick Cromwell could not possibly have inflicted more than superficial damage.

The castle was leased recently as a conference centre but it is still owned by the Borthwick family.

Bothwell Castle

Lanark, Strathclyde (9 miles south-east of Glasgow).

Historic Scotland, open to the public.

Bothwell is the finest of Scotland's 13th-century castles. It stands on a rocky promontory on the Clyde, a mile to the west of old Bothwell Bridge and near to Bothwell village.

It is similar to the English and French castles of the same period and is one of the largest stone castles in Scotland. Its red sandstone walls are 15 feet thick and, at the side facing the river, are 60 feet high in parts. The corners are protected by (the remains of) round or square towers and a mighty-looking round donjon or keep dominates the rest. Interestingly, the donjon bears a resemblance to the massive cylindrical great tower at Coucy in France (demolished in 1916).

The donjon stands on the *enceinte* and is separated from the courtyard by its own ditch and parapet. This was the original part of the castle, built around 1270 by Walter de Moravia (the name became Moray then, later, Murray). Its walls are 15 feet thick and rise 90 feet to the top of the parapet. It is 65 feet in diameter and, despite the cylindrical exterior, is octagonal internally. Much of the interior, however, has been destroyed. The basement of the donjon, entered by a newel stair, was

undoubtedly once a store. There is also a well there, half sunk into the wall.

The floor above is the hall. It was 37 feet in diameter and 22 feet high to the apex of the vault. The vault, supported by moulded ribs resting on corbels, was probably timber. The tracery of the window facing the court still remains.

The entrance is on the hall floor, 3 feet above the floor level. The entrance passage has been skilfully zig-zagged to enhance defence. A portcullis was worked from the room above, as was the drawbridge. The newel stair also provides access to the above floors and once led to the parapet, since demolished. The intermediate floors may have housed the garrison and the top storey where the lord and his family resided. There was almost certainly a guardroom at the top of the stair, higher than the parapet.

A mural door from the donjon led to the garderobes in the south curtain. Strong defensive doors on narrow passages link the donjon from its two upper floors to the south curtain wall parapet connecting with the adjoining tower. It eventually connects with a postern escape gate in the southern wall, itself defended by a portcullis.

Much destruction and restoration have taken place in the castle, so much so that it is difficult to date the rebuilding and additions made to the basic 13th-century plan. Some damage must have occurred during the English occupation of 1298–9, when the Scots beseiged it for more than 14 months. During that period Wallace's men attacked and retook Bothwell, and more damage would have been inflicted in 1301 when Edward I captured it with an army of 6800 men. In order to take the castle, the English king had to employ a variety of siege apparatus and weapons, including a huge moveable, covered tower. It was manufactured in Glasgow and took thirty waggons two days to move its prefabricated parts nine miles.

It is likely that the English held Bothwell for the next 13 years, though — during that time — it may have fallen to a second Scottish assault, only to have been retaken once again. But, after Bruce's great victory at Bannockburn the castle reverted to the Scots until the early 1330s.

A period of restoration took place in 1336 when Edward III made Bothwell his headquarters for a month or so. However, there was further demolition in 1337 when its owner, Sir Andrew de Moray, the Warden of Scotland, recaptured it. He set about demolishing the building in accordance with Robert Bruce's famous 'Testament' which urged the Scots to destroy their castles and rely on a 'scorched earth' policy to defend their lands. Apparently the castle then lay derelict till it was taken over by 'Black Archibald the Grim', 3rd Earl of Douglas and Lord of Galloway, who set about restoring it. He rebuilt the hall and chapel and erected a new wall from east to west. Further work was carried out in the 15th and 16th centuries.

Surrounded by trees on the slopes beneath the base of its south and west sides (the trees stand on the north and east banks of that part of the Clyde which bends around the castle), Bothwell is a splendid and substantial ruin. The outline of the base of the towers to the north side indicates how enormous this castle was when complete.

Braemar Castle

Deiside, Grampian

Privately owned, open to the public.

Braemar Castle is out of place in a Highland setting. Standing on a hill above the upper River Dee, this 17th-century *L*-plan structure looks like a prison or something from a film set. This is due to the longish, wide turrets and the semi-circular tower almost clustered together, rising behind a star-shaped curtain in the foreground. It is crenellated according to Renaissance theories of fortification. (Although the tower and turrets are fairly close together, and crenellated, containing vertical lines of windows, Braemar Castle is still remarkably dour-looking.)

As it was used after the 1745 rising as part of a plan by the government to subdue the Highlands, the building was fortified and turned into a military barracks. The upper works were altered at this time and crenellations replaced the conical roofs of the turrets. This, of course, also adds to the feel of falseness — although the crenellations were added for quite practical reasons of outlook and musket fire.

Braemar Castle was built in 1628 by John Erskine, Earl of Mar, as a counterbalance to the rising power of the Farquharsons. In 1689, however, it was seized and burnt by the Jacobite 'Black Colonel' John Farquharson of Inverey. It was to stand for 50 years afterwards as a burnt-out shell.

Inside the castle the dungeons and living rooms are still quite apparent. One can still see the graffiti carved by bored English soldiers on some of the walls.

Braemar village plays host to the famous Highland Games on the first Saturday of September every year. As Braemar is normally full of tourists around this period, this may not be the best time for castle enthusiasts to visit.

Brodick Castle

Isle of Arran, Strathclyde

National Trust for Scotland, open to the public.

The original structure dates from the time of the Norse occupation of the Isle of Arran, on which the present Brodick Castle stands. Some of the stones in the lower storeys of the tower ·at the eastern end are believed to date from Robert Bruce's time. The historian John of Fordun records that there were two castles on Arran in the 14th century, one of these being, undoubtedly, Brodick.

At first sight it looks like a 19th-century castle, as the most prominent western part is, indeed, of that time. This part of the castle was designed by James Gillespie Graham who was commissioned in 1844 to build it to comply with the earlier design. Also, from not too far a distance, it blends with the rest of the castle thus giving the impression already mentioned. This is due to the use of the same red Arran sandstone as that employed in the earlier sections.

The old castle is a main block lying east–west. The join with the 19th-century building is quite visible on the south front where longer first-floor windows and higher second-floor ones begin. Indeed, the south side of the old castle also looks as if it was built at two different stages as the eastern windows are higher than the western ones and there is a change of pattern in the parapet. It is

also broken on the eastern side by two dormer windows. The old block also has an attic. To the north are two stair towers, unusually, joined. One is corbelled out to the square above second floor level and has the parapet continuing around it; it is topped with a cap-house. The other is square and has joined to it a slightly taller (crow-stepped) gable tower. Further north is an extended lower battery, also crow-stepped, added in the 17th century. This is approached by a stone forestair that once led to Brodick's original entrance, probably replacing a movable timber stair. The entrance is now through the 19th-century building.

Brodick was granted to James, Lord Hamilton, with the title Earl of Arran, by his cousin James IV. The Hamiltons became marquises in 1599 and dukes in 1648, amassing great wealth through coal. The direct line died out with the Duchess of Montrose, daughter of the 12th Duke of Hamilton. In 1958 the castle was given to the National Trust for Scotland.

Brodie Castle

Forres Moray, Grampian

National Trust for Scotland, open to the public.

The Brodie family owned the castle which takes
their surname till 1982. The castle, standing north
of the village of Brodie, dates from the 15th
century, with additions in the 16th century. Its
nucleus may go back to the 12th century; Brodies
have owned it since the 11th century. In 1645, Lord
Lewis Gordon burned the building while leading
Montrose's northern campaign for Charles I.
Disastrously, all of the archives were destroyed,
depriving the Brodies and the rest of the neigh-
bourhood of their genealogical and historical
records. One solitary document survived: a
missive from Robert the Bruce referring to the
property of Dyke. (A Pictish stone was found on
this Dyke property and now stands in one of the
castle drives.) Though it appears that all the
plasterwork of the great hall was ruined beyond
repair by the fire, the ceiling of the blue room
escaped damage. The rebuilding of the surviving
parts took place in the 17th and 18th centuries.

The result of the rebuilding and additions was a
Z-plan castle with corbelled and crenellated
parapets at the towers. The four-storey rectangular block, with a parapet walk drained by cannon
spouts, was built during the first phase. The
present castle consists of this tower — now at the
south-west corner — together with large extensions added to the east, north and north-east in
1824. These are neo-Tudor and are the work of
William Burn. The castle was in need of much
repair after a fire in 1786 which, after causing a
great deal of damage to fabric, asphyxiated the
laird's wife. In 1846, James Wylson remodelled the
curvilinear neo-Tudor gables with crow-steps.

The kitchen to the north and the vaulted
basement rooms are very possibly the oldest
internal parts of Brodie Castle. One of the tower's
first floor rooms — the aforementioned blue
room — contains post-Union of the Crowns plas-

19

terwork. The ceiling of the dining room is a massively enriched plasterwork of the same date. The decoration, like most of the interior, is by Burn. Wylson reconstructed the ground floor, adding the enormous crypt-like entrance hall and neo-classical library. The drawing room, displaying decorative stencilling, was recently restored.

The red drawing room — originally the old hall — is now virtually a gallery. It contains several portraits and works by various 17th-century Dutch masters.

The corbelled mantelpiece is split in two at the centre with a Gothic figure in between, itself standing on a corbel. Above the mantelpiece are two rows of niches reaching to the ceiling — the niches on the top row being double the width of the ones beneath — containing statues. At either side of the lower fireplace is a niche in which stands a statue. Above those are two statues mounted on pillars. They are under Gothic-style canopies which are immediately beneath the ceiling.

Home to a fine collection of Flemish, Dutch and English paintings, Brodie is not so much a fortalice as a country house. Owned by the National Trust for Scotland since 1982, it still retains a family flat. It is the seat of one of the oldest untitled landed families in the UK. The head is addressed simply as 'Brodie'.

Caerlaverock Castle

Dumfries and Galloway

Historic Scotland, open to the public.

The ruins of Caerlaverock Castle stand near the mouth of the River Nith, 7 miles south-east of Dumfries. The general appearance of the structure is one of sombre desolation. It stands in a moat surrounded by what was formerly marshland and was obviously once a formidable fortress. For one thing, it would have been impossible to approach it as an enemy from any direction without putting oneself in grave danger due to it being surrounded by water and marsh for a considerable distance. Woods to the south would have slowed down an enemy. The views from the enormous walls gave the defenders plenty of warning as well as secure protection. The surging tide of the Solway was an additional water defence.

Caerlaverock is triangular — a unique design in Scotland — with towers at each corner. Though one is all but demolished, the others are almost complete. The strongly defensive gatehouse to the north — the most impressive in Scotland — is a massive double drum tower behind which two of the other walls meet. This has a portcullis room above the entrance. Known locally as the 'Island of

Caerlaverock', it is entered by a wooden bridge in lieu of the original drawbridge. Its earliest parts date from around 1290. So many additions were made that it includes masonry of every period between the 13th and 17th centuries.

Most likely built as a bridgehead against the eventuality of a sea-based English invasion, the castle saw much war-like activity. In spite of its formidable appearance and defensive advantages, it was besieged and taken by Edward I soon after its completion. Soon after Edward II's accession, the Keeper, Sir Eustace Maxwell, declared for Robert Bruce. Shortly afterwards, the castle was besieged but it held out. Before long, though, it was another victim of Bruce's 'scorched earch' policy.

Much of the present building was constructed around 1347. Murdoch's tower was added (so called because Murdoch, Duke of Albany, was said to have been imprisoned there).

Some records maintain that Roger Kirkpatrick wrecked Caerlaverock in 1355 or 1356. They also maintain that he was killed there but these records are insufficient evidence historically. It is certain that the castle was partly destroyed, but only after Kirkpatrick's death. There is a theory that it was deserted for two generations. This is based on the existence of another medieval site a short way south, supposedly the residence of Caerlaverock lords after their main castle had been gutted.

Other additions were made in the 1400s, especially in the central part of the west curtain and in the western tower of the gatehouse. According to one historian, the bartisan of Caerlaverock was completed around 1460 by the 2nd Lord Maxwell. This is quite possible as the parapets on the gatehouse, the one on Murdoch's tower, and the additions to the front and rear of the gatehouse, all appear to be of 15th-century origin. (It was the additions to the latter that turned it into a tower house.)

The English are reputed to have caused it much damage in the 16th century. There is no evidence of this but it would seem likely, as much construction work was done on Caerlaverock in 1593. A new block of Renaissance-style buildings was added around 1634 by its owner, Lord Nithsdale. This three-storey residence was built against the inner face of the eastern wall, to contrast with the medieval features. About six years after its erection, the castle held out for the king against the Covenanters. The siege lasted for about three months.

Castle Campbell

Dollar, Clackmannanshire

National Trust for Scotland and under guardianship of Historic Scotland, open to the public.

Castle Campbell stands a mile north of — and high above — the picturesque town of Dollar. It is surrounded by other even higher Ochil hills, some of which are forested. The situation is one of the most beautiful of all Scottish castles — the stuff of romance. Some of the best views and walks in central Scotland are in the immediate vicinity of this impressive citadel.

There are two routes up to the castle: the steep main road and a rocky track. The latter is through a woodland ravine, some of the most precipitous parts being covered by railed wooden catwalks. A burn runs its length, breaking into a waterfall at one point.

On approaching from the *top* car park (there is another at the foot of the main road), Castle Campbell rises abruptly on a spur above the surrounding forestry, looking quite awesome beneath the adjacent Ochils.

The courtyard is entered by an arched pend to the north, once bridged by a gatehouse. To the west stands the 15th-century oblong tower with sheer walls rising to an overhanging parapet 60 feet above the ground. From each of the floors — or from the upper levels of its staircase — is a breathtaking view over the Devon valley southwards to the plains of the Forth. The best view is from the parapet but, due to the castle's giddy situation, the impression is that one is much higher than 60 feet above the courtyard. It demands a head for heights.

The first floor is entered through a later stair tower adjoining the east range. (The original stair was in the opposite wall. The other entrance is an arched doorway in the west wall on the first storey. It is ascended to by modern wooden stairs, in place of the original movable stair.) This floor is vaulted and, in a neuk in the east wall, there is a thoroughly unpleasant prison, reached through a hatch in the stone floor.

The second floor is the only unvaulted one in the tower. Within the walls is an L-shaped latrine chamber housing a seat, chute and a recess for a wall lamp.

The third floor is covered by a barrel vault supporting the roof of the tower above. This vault is embellished with an intricate system of transverse ribs, crossed by ridge ribs, running from end to end. On the underside of the vault are two carved or cast grotesque masks. They probably served as centrepieces for lamps. As they are Renaissance style, it would suggest that this vault was added during the late 16th or early 17th century.

The west part of the building, adjoining the tower, is French Renaissance style. It is of smoother ashlar than the tower and is built over a double-arched loggia. The loggia leads into the public toilet and tea room. Behind its ruins can be seen a 16th-century part in coarse rubble.

The ruins to the south of the courtyard also offer splendid views over to the Forth plains. A similar panorama can be enjoyed from the three-tiered terrace gardens beneath. They are entered through an arched pend with a stepped, cobbled floor.

The under part of the south range ruins has three small cellars — there is public admittance to two — which, with their very low vaulted ceilings, are quite claustrophobic. This recalls to mind its original name: Castle Gloom. There appears to be nothing on record saying how it came to receive this appellation. Interestingly enough, the castle stands where the Burns of Sorrow and Care join. The nearest town, Dollar, is thought by some place-name enthusiasts to come from the middle English *dolour* — distress or sadness. Did some tragic event occur in the area lost to historical record?

Castle Fraser

Inverurie, Aberdeen, Grampian

National Trust for Scotland, open to the public.

One of the most outstanding examples of castle building in Scotland, Castle Fraser was largely the work of two famous masons, James Leiper and I Bell.

The first Fraser to own the land on which the castle now stands was Thomas, who by charter of James II exchanged his lands of Cornton in Stirlingshire for Muchal-in-Mar, as these Fraser lands were then called. It is thought that the original structure that he built is incorporated in the present one. The first builder of the present structure was probably the 5th laird, Michael Fraser, circa the late 1500s or early 1600s. It was *his* son, Andrew, who completed the Z-plan.

The main building rises to four storeys including the attic, the four windows of which have carved triangular pediments with finials on each apex. There is a bartisan on the top left-hand corner and one on the corner adjacent to and behind it. Under the attic windows runs elaborate corbelling with imitation cannon spouts. The main door is within a recessed archway and has a fanlight window.

To the right and joined to this block is the castle's most salient feature, the great round

27

tower. It has a flat roof surrounded by a balustrade. This is reached by a stairwell with an ogee-roofed cap-house. This looks like a bartisan and is between the tower and the main block. The corbelling of this stairwell rises to meet the staggered corbelling separating the tower's top three storeys from the bottom four.

The last Fraser died childless in 1897. The building remained empty until 1922 when it was bought by Viscount Cowdrey.

In 1976, this magnificent building was donated to the National Trust for Scotland.

Cawdor Castle

Nairn, Highland

Privately owned, open to the public.

Six miles south-west of Nairn, set near the shores
of the Moray Firth, stands Cawdor Castle. Dom-
inating the village of the same name, it is quite
impressive to view from the road above the
surrounding ditch. A first sighting is of the oldest
part of the castle, the central tower keep (c.1454)
rising dramatically behind the drawbridge wall.
This wall is joined on either side by 17th-century
buildings. Each has a corbelled bartisan—or
pepperpot turret—at their top corners to the left
and right of the drawbridge. They complement the
bartisans on the four top corners of the keep that
protrude from the crenellated parapet. The keep's
were originally open-roofed but were raised in the
17th century and given conical roofs like those on
the front buildings.

Originally, the keep stood alone above the deep
dry ditch and was, as now, reached by a drawbridge. It is four storeys high and has a garret.
Formerly, the entrance was at first floor level and

was approached by a movable timber stair but it is now at basement level. The basement itself is vaulted, as is the third floor. A straight stair in the north wall connects the basement and hall. This had a mural chamber and was also originally vaulted in stone to prevent the tower from being burnt out from below.

The first major extensions were carried out in the 16th century when a curtain wall and further living accommodation were added. In the 17th century the north and west wings were enlarged to form a courtyard on the keep's north side. Stables and domestic offices occupied the south. A great deal of mural carving was also executed.

There are several impressive Renaissance fireplaces worth seeing. One is decorated with a monkey blowing a horn, a cat playing a fiddle and a mermaid playing a harp. Its most curious decoration, though, is a fox smoking a pipe —considering the date on the fireplace: 1511. (The earliest record of tobacco arriving in Europe is 1558 when Phillip II of Spain received the plant as a present.) The fireplace commemorates the marriage of Muriel Calder to Sir John Campbell, the third son of the 2nd Earl of Argyll. This happened around 1510 when the castle became Campbell property. The Campbells had had their eyes on the Calder estate for some time. In 1499 Campbell of Argyll had ordered the kidnapping of Muriel Calder from her guardian by Campbell of Inverliver. This enterprise was at the cost of the lives of all six of Inverliver's sons.

The castle was uninhabited for 100 years after the 1745 rising when its Campbell lairds moved to family lands in Wales. The castle has remained virtually untouched since then.

Claypotts Castle

Dundee, Tayside

Historic Scotland, open to the public.

Claypotts Castle rises almost abruptly among surrounding modern bungalows in the Dundee suburb of Broughty Ferry. It can be seen clearly from the roundabout where the roads to Dundee and Arbroath meet. Though it has a rough rubble facade it is a particularly neat structure (it had a facelift in 1984) probably due to its compactness. Its groundspace is not much more than that of the average cottage. One can walk around it in less than a minute.

Similar to the Z-plan Terpersie, the main round tower has a garret with crow-step gables and a dormer window, similar to the garret on the tower at the opposite end. The bottom corners of both garrets protrude over the towers. The effect on each is like a cottage placed on a stone cylinder. Though these garrets, or watch rooms, look similar, they are of slightly different dimensions. One was built a generation later than the other.

The slates on the roof are dowelled — an old

method of pegging—clearly seen from the inside. Though from inside the light can be seen through them, this amazing technique still prevents rain from getting through.

The various sizes of windows—some minute—dotted seemingly at random across the castle face give it a quaint charm.

The earliest known reference to Claypotts occurs in a document of 1365. The next known reference is not until the beginning of the 16th century when the lands were 'held of the Abbot of Lindores by a lay tenant, John Strachan'. Strachan's descendants held the castle till 1601 when they moved to Balunie and sold it to Sir William Graham of Claverhouse for 12 000 marks. David Strachan, who sold Claypotts, was the last owner actually to live there. The last Graham to hold the lands was the most famous: John, Viscount Dundee and Earl of Claverhouse—the latter title given to him in 1688 for his services to James VII. Immortalized by Sir Walter Scott as 'Bonnie Dundee', though called 'Bluiddy Claver'se' by the Covenanters, he was killed the following year at Killiecrankie, after which the lands were declared forfeit and reverted to the Crown. They passed to the Douglases in 1694, to their relations the Homes in 1827, and to the Commissioner of Works in 1926. The castle is now run by Historic Scotland.

Corgarff Castle

Aberdeen, Grampian

Historic Scotland, open to the public.

Corgarff Castle stands on a height at the end of the Lecht Pass — frequently blocked by winter snows — facing the steep brae above Cockbridge. This four-storey tower was built around 1537 as a hunting seat for Thomas Erskine, Earl of Mar. Since 1435 the lands had been annexed by the Crown, as had the estates belonging to the Earldom, but in 1507 the forest of Corgarff with some other Mar lands was granted to Alexander, later 1st Lord Elphinstone, by James IV.

Oblong in plan, with its original staircase carried a storey higher to provide a cap-house on the south-east angle, it replaced the structure destroyed in 1581. This was when the Forbes laird's wife, Margaret Campbell, her family and servants were all burned alive in a feud with the Gordons. Adam Gordon of Auchindoon, or one of his men, removed the ground wall stone of the garderobe chute and inserted fire up the flue. This tragic event is recorded in the old ballad *Edom o' Gordon*.

Though restored when the Erskines recovered the lands from the Forbeses, the Jacobites burnt it

again in 1689. It was besieged and taken in 1746 by Lord Ancrum's men. Lord Mar forfeited the lands passing them back to the Forbeses. It was restored again in 1748 when the government bought it for use as a Hanoverian post for disarming the Highlands. At that stage, wings were added to each gable wall and a star-shaped loophole curtain, similar to the one at Braemar, was erected.

Originally the castle was built as a tower house, with two vaulted cellars in the basement, a high vaulted hall on the first floor with an adjoining kitchen and upper storey and garret. After the fires in 1581 and 1689, most of the castle still stood intact — except, obviously, for the wooden floors and the roof.

Craigievar Castle

Near Aberdeen, Grampian

National Trust for Scotland, open to the public.

Craigievar Castle is the archetypical Scottish fortified house. This *L*-plan tower house, almost fairy-tale in appearance, is enhanced by its setting in secluded countryside south of Alford. The first references to the estate are on a charter of 1457, still on display in the castle, naming the Mortimers as the owners. They started to build the castle towards the end of the 16th century but, due to financial difficulties, sold the property to a flamboyant merchant, William Forbes, who made a fortune trading with the Baltic ports.

The top two storeys of Craigievar — three in the case of the central rectangular tower — are distinguished from the bottom four by staggered corbelling. The central tower, with its flat balustraded roof, is embedded in the *L*. The simpli-

city of the tower is as dramatic a contrast to the riot of conically capped bartisans, corbelled gables, ogee-roofed cap-houses and balustrades as the ornamentally elaborate upper floors are to the plainer lower ones.

The exuberance of this architectural display matches the integrity of the design lavished on the restricted interior space. This can be entered only through the main arched doorway at the foot of the rectangular tower. The studded outer door has an iron yett behind and a studded double door on the stone stair leading to the great hall. The hall — described by one expert as 'one of the most remarkable rooms in Scotland' — is entered through a door in a wooden screen. It is carved with classical arches topped by a Renaissance balustrade above which is a minstrel's gallery, now divided in two. The ceiling with its groined vault is particularly intricate. Foliage, classical and biblical portrait medallions and elaborate pendants adorn its shafts and a huge heraldic tablet between two Renaissance pilasters stretches from the mantel-piece to the arches of the ceiling.

Next to the hall is the withdrawing room with a plaster ceiling, dated 1625, and wall panelling of Memel pine. One of the panels is a disguised door that leads into a tiny room. This is situated in the rectangular tower. (In most other castles of the period the tower was round and contained a newel stair. It was one of the achievements of Craigievar's architect that he found room for stairs elsewhere.)

The chamber above the hall is the Queen's Room. This contains a double bed with a rococo-looking headboard and a curtained canopy, both of which reach to the low, elaborately plastered ceiling. Two large portraits adorn the walls above the fireplace. These are the most delightful parts of a most delightful castle. The view from the tower roof is its crowning glory.

Craigmillar Castle

Edinburgh, Midlothian

Historic Scotland, open to the public.

The imposing ruins of Craigmillar Castle stand just beyond Duddingston on the southern outskirts of Edinburgh. Suburbs surround this famous castle but the new buildings are at least a decent distance from the irregular rocky ridge on which it stands.

Though it is basically an *L*-shaped structure, it is quite an elaborate building. Built about 1374, the central tower—53 feet by 49 feet on the longest sides—is constructed of close-textured, reddish-grey rubble. In 1427, a 30-foot machicolated curtain wall with circular angular towers was built around the tower house. It is the best-preserved example of its kind in Scotland. The ridge, which falls away from the base of the tower into a steep cliff, was obviously chosen with the enhancement of defence in mind. An attempt at walking around the castle verifies this! The north-eastern tower, which faced the main approach to Craigmillar Castle, is the only one provided with cannon openings. They resemble inverted keyholes. The rest of the wall was serviced by large round openings, high in the towers, for large guns. An additional walled enclosure complete with moat

was added in the 16th century. The building is entered through a wide, arched doorway over which is a carving depicting the Preston arms. Overhead, on the battlements, is a lion rampant. This emblazonment of the kings of Scotland was a special concession to the Lord of Craigmillar who, as tenant-in-chief, was entitled to place it above his own arms.

The vaulted lobby leads to a turnpike and also gives access to dingy cellars entered by doors placed there at a much later date. One inner door closes the cellars while another shuts off the turnpike. The hall on the first storey is 35 feet by 21 feet. On the wall opposite the entrance is a richly moulded fireplace with lintels resting on moulded shafts. Next to the fireplace a door opens into a small privy which is now a passage leading to the later buildings. The hall also contains three large windows with stone seats. During the 16th or 17th century they were altered to have leaded glass inserted into the upper sections and wooden shutters fitted below. At the hall's north-east corner is a mural closet. Some experts think it may have been built over a pit prison.

Where the stair from the basement reaches the hall is a landing. On the side opposite the hall is another stair which carries on up to the roof. This divided stair—that is, these two separate flights—was planned as a defence measure but had the added advantage of leaving space in the wing free for three private rooms. The room at the hall level had been a kitchen originally but was made into a living room at a later date when a newer kitchen was built.

Various additions were made over the centuries. After the castle was burnt in 1544, the east range was added. This included a private room, bedchambers, a kitchen and cellars. The western range was reconstructed in 1661, designed differently to the usual 17th-century castle wing. The dining room, the withdrawing room and the kitchen were all on the ground floor, opening into one another without a corridor.

Though of great significance architecturally,

Craigmillar Castle is of even more interest historically. In 1544 it was partially destroyed by the
English. In 1566 Mary, Queen of Scots retreated
here from the intrigues of Holyrood after Rizzio's
murder. Soon after, the conspirators signed their
famous 'bond' here before murdering Darnley.
The queen was in residence at the time and it is
therefore likely that she was involved in the
plot—especially as she was known to be having
an amorous liaison with Bothwell at the time.
During the civil war of 1572, Mar garrisoned
Craigmillar. In 1660, Sir John Gilmour bought the
barony from the Prestons. A descendant gave the
castle to the then Scottish Development Department in 1946.

Crathes Castle

Banchory, Kincardine and Deeside

National Trust for Scotland, open to the public.

After Craigievar, Crathes Castle is surely the finest surviving continuously occupied late-16th-century tower house in Scotland. According to tradition, Alexander Burnet (the name was originally Burnard and, later, Burnett) began in 1553 to build the L-plan stronghold. It was not completed till the time of the 12th laird, Alexander's great-grandson, in 1596. That was when the Bells — a family of renowned Aberdeen masons — reconstructed the upper parts. The beginnings of this Scottish baronial castle are commemorated by two shields over the east wall doorway. One contains the impaled arms of the Burnetts and the Hamiltons, with the date of commencement, while the other contains the monograms AB and JG with the date of completion.

 The upper parts, reminiscent of Craigievar, are a riot of round and square corbelled bartisans, string courses, gabling and gargoyles. The lower storeys, also like Craigievar's, are much plainer; though a late-Victorian Renaissance-style window was inserted at first floor level.

The rounded corners made it difficult for besiegers to knock out the cornerstones and weaken the structure. It also tapers towards the top. The original purpose for that kind of structure was to render it difficult for an enemy to shelter underneath the battlements while assaulting the castle. But Crathes was built this way for aesthetic reasons. There was, however, besides the usual iron yett, a tripping-stone on the turnpike. An enemy ascending the stair would unexpectedly find the eleventh step adjusted, causing him to fall.

Crathes Castle has an unusual plan. The main block is double pile due to the inclusion of the stair, its enormous width is spanned by a double-ridged roof, the valley of which stands out on the south face via a turret corbelled out at the second floor.

The upper floors are worth seeing, if only to view the brightly painted Jacobean ceilings. There is one in the Chamber of the Nine Nobles, depicting ancient warriors of antiquity on the ceiling boards between the joists. The Chamber of the Muses' ceiling is illustrated with medieval-looking musicians and the joists either side of them are decorated with Celtic and Jacobean patterns. On the sides of the joists are maxims, jingles and explanations of the pictures.

The Green Lady's Room is worth a visit, as is the impressive first floor. This vaulted tower room was originally the great hall. It contains an Elizabethan fireplace built with solid granite.

The basement of Crathes is vaulted and contained the usual kitchen and cellars, the wine cellar having the customary service stair to the hall directly above. The hall stands over the western cellars. (These have a plastered semi-circular vault with painted decoration at the arched recesses and on the under surfaces of the window architraves.) Its most salient feature is a 16th-century caryatid chimney piece, imported from Italy in the 1870s.

The 11th baronet added a somewhat incongruous late-Victorian wing overlooking the upper garden. It was destroyed by fire in 1966 and has never been restored.

The magnificent 18th-century gardens include some of Britain's finest plant collections. The Irish yew hedges are over 200 years old and the lime avenues are possibly older.

Crichton Castle

Crichton, Lothian

Historic Scotland, open to the public.

Crichton Castle is an immensely interesting ruin architecturally as well as historically. It is no small surprise that Sir Walter Scott admired the building. He celebrated it in *Marmion*:

> The courtyard's graceful portico;
> Above its cornice row and row,
> Of fair hewn facets, richly show
> Their pointed diamond form.

Even its situation is interesting. It stands majestically on a hillock almost at the head of the East Lothian River Tyne, two miles south of Pathhead.

It is entered from the east side through a pend — originally part of an oblong three-storey gatehouse. It was built in the early 15th century by the Lord Chancellor Crichton to further fortify the keep to its north. The gatehouse is part of another keep to the south, running westwards, which has its own great and upper halls on the first and second floors.

Beneath the hall of the north keep is a vaulted basement, lit by narrow loops. A narrow loft in the basement served as a pit prison known as Massle More. On the north-west corner of the first floor is a newel stair, leading to the second storey. It would have led to the upper floors before they were demolished. The walls of this keep are seven feet thick. Only the ruins of the lower part of the hall remain. The north tower was partly destroyed in 1445 but reconstructed at a later date.

Going through the gatehouse pend, the visitor arrives in the courtyard. Straight ahead is the looming ruin of the west wing. This three-storey building was erected in the second half of the 15th century, but with a round six-storey tower at the south-west angle. Behind the towers were bedrooms. The adjacent first and second floors were kitchens. To the right of that, running back to meet the north keep, is the most pleasant part of the interior. A Romanesque arcade runs under the 'diamond-studded' Florentine arcade of this north wing, completing the courtyard extension. This arcade, and the diamond facade, turns at a right-angle to join the western range. At this point it is one arch wide. The arches give it the feel of an abbey cloister. The diamond masonry is slightly reminiscent of tyre tread. On sunny days it becomes a great pattern of sharp shadows to resemble strongly a 1960s op art painting. As these shadows change with the earth's movement, in the same way the shadow on a sundial's face does, the wall can thus be compared to an enormous kinetic sculpture. It is truly an architectural wonder of 16th-century Scotland. This facade was built by the bastard grandson of James Francis Stewart, the notorious Earl of Bothwell. Though well-known as a ruffian, he had outstandingly good taste. No doubt the time he had spent in Italy civilized him. This part of the courtyard is said to be built after the manner of the Palazzo dei Diamante at Ferrara. It may be the work of an Italian architect whom Bothwell brought back to Scotland with him when he returned in 1581. His countess, Margaret Douglas, was apparently as much involved in this addition as he was. Their initials and an anchor engraved on the north wing attest to this. Internally, the cellars in the ground floor of the north wing were rearranged to improve the kitchen facilities. East of the kitchen, the Bothwells provided a well-lit dining room with a handsome fireplace and buffet.

Bothwell does not seem to have been concerned about preserving the original tower. For many years architectural historians failed to recognize its importance—so much so that they considered the tower in the south-west angle to be the nucleus of the castle.

A little to the south of Crichton Castle stands a roofless building with massive buttresses. This is not a chapel, as one would expect, but a stable. Aptly, a horseshoe window is above the door. There were also grooms' quarters on the ground floor.

The earliest record of Crichton estates are on a

13th-century charter when Robert III presented John de Crichton with the barony of Crichton. Possibly he began building the north tower—which, after the addition of the north wing, makes it look more as if to the east. Some historians consider his son, the famous Sir William Crichton, to have been the one most likely to have done so and to have added the keep gatehouse in the 15th century. (This is the James Crichton who, in 1440, lured the young Earl Douglas and his brother to Edinburgh Castle. They were murdered at the signal of a pig's head being brought to the table. This famous incident is known as the Black Dinner.)

The castle was to have a history of lords and occupants who were not of the most upright character. In 1483, the 3rd Lord Crichton was incarcerated in the castle for his part in the Duke of Albany's conspiracy against James III. Though he managed to escape, the king seized his lands and castle, giving them to Sir John Ramsay. Ironically, Sir John, who became the 1st Lord Bothwell, died an 'obscure and traitorous spy' for the English after Sauchieburn. At this, James IV forfeited the estate and presented it to Patrick Hepburn, who was made Earl Bothwell. In 1569, the castle was forfeited for the third time when James Hepburn, the most notorious Earl Bothwell, was found guilty of conspiracy against the Crown.

Mary, Queen of Scots, his mistress and later wife, visited the castle occasionally. She is reputed to have attended a wedding there in 1572, for one of her many illegitimate half-brothers. It is also reckoned that she spent part of her honeymoon there with Darnley. The initials M S D are cut into the stone above the two central pillars on the east side of the courtyard. Do they stand for Mary Stuart Darnley? If it is true that she spent her honeymoon there, it seems to be a cruel twist of fate that she would later be married to Crichton's lord who was involved in her previous husband's murder.

Culzean Castle

12 miles south of Ayr, Strathclyde

National Trust for Scotland, open to the public.

On a high cliff overlooking the lower Firth of
Clyde, enhancing its magnificence, stands stately
Culzean Castle. On a clear day, it has a view of
Kintyre and the mountains of Arran.

The original building was a medieval keep which
stood on a site associated for many centuries with
the clan Kennedy. Apparently the keep was a
round tower with a single room in each floor, all
connected by a newel stair on a projecting tower.
Much of it had been demolished in the late 17th
century and replaced by a more comfortable
dwelling. It was about the period of the 'Glorious
Revolution' when Culzean (pronounced Cul-ain)
was rebuilt. We know that it had 'pretty gardens
and orchards, adorned with excellent terraces,
and with walls laden with peaches, apricots,
cherries and other fruits' as the minister of nearby
Maybole wrote in 1693.

The present Georgian building is the work of

Robert Adam, the most popular architect of his day, whose influence spread to Russia in the east and America in the west. He was employed by David Kennedy, the 10th Earl of Cassellis, who inherited the title from his brother in 1775. David Kennedy had spent some time in Italy where he had developed a passion for Renaissance architecture.

One of the particular achievements of Adam was that he presented much of what was already there. His other great achievement was that on completion the new parts looked as if they had been conceived with the old.

The 17th-century house had rooms added on either side to create a symmetrical front. This was common practice in the Georgian period. Though the large windows were of classical design, they were surrounded by corner turrets with croslet windows. These turrets, like the rest of the building, were crenellated. The result looks almost Victorian.

The work, begun in 1777, also involved the demolition of the 9th earl's modest block—which stood on the cliff edge—and some other outbuildings. In their place stands the round tower which houses the circular room. (The 9th earl, Thomas—something of a pragmatist—was more interested in agriculture than the elegance of his family seat. The purpose of *his* building was solely to serve the needs of the farm. He introduced crop rotation and green crops for the winter feeding of cattle. He imported bulls and horses and drastically diminished the area's sheep. He also enclosed his lands with dykes and hedges which involved the removal of smaller tenants.) The saloon, as it is called, was restored in 1968 to Adam's original design. The floor is covered by a reddish-coloured circular carpet—the centre of which is directly under the centre of a crystal chandelier. The carpet, a copy of Adam's original, was woven locally at Irvine. The panelled doors of varnished natural wood have corniced lintels over which hang gilt-framed oil paintings. Between the doors are arched niches in which stand urns on tripod-like stands.

Adam placed his final masterpiece — the oval staircase — in what had been a dark and damp courtyard at the back of the tower house. It rises from the ground floor up to the first storey which is surrounded by Corinthian pillars supporting the second. These in turn have pillars directly above them over the oval entablature holding up the third floor. Light from the stairway's glass dome reaches to the foot of the red-carpeted stair.

Adam was not content with building merely a stately castle for gracious living. He built a home farm to the north of the castle. A quadrangle with turreted corners led into the courtyard, which was surrounded by open archways leading to the other buildings. It had fallen into dilapidation and, as it was felt that it had to be adapted to fulfil the needs of a park centre, skilled masons worked on it between 1971–4.

Culzean Castle has an Eisenhower exhibition room. This contains the desk at which General Eisenhower planned the North Africa landing, among other personal mementoes. When he was US president, the National Trust offered him the top flat as a permanent Scottish home.

This remarkable castle boasts other attractions such as a deer park, woodland walks, a swan pond, a theatre, lecture rooms and various natural history exhibitions.

Dirleton Castle

East Lothian, Lothian

*National Trust for Scotland and under guard-
ianship of Historic Scotland, open to the public.*

Dirleton Castle rises abruptly above the neat,
almost level, park of the village of the same name.
(Dirleton has the reputation of being the prettiest
village in Scotland.) It was originally built in the
13th century by the De Vaux family to be besieged
in 1298 by Anthony Beck, Edward I's warrior
Bishop of Durham. Though he inflicted much
damage, it was rebuilt after the Scots captured it in
1311. In 1650 its garrison of Border freebooters was
defeated by Cromwell's troops. On surrender,
three of the leaders were hanged from its walls.

The old castle was crammed on to a restricted
site, making a triangular court. A later addition was
forced to conform to the contour of the rock. Its
position was further strengthened by a surrounding deep moat, at least 50 feet wide. Like the
entrance gateway the moat is well preserved. It
was spanned by a movable wooden bridge that
rested on piers. It was further defended by a
drawbridge.

It is still entered by a long wooden drawbridge
(not the original) over wooden criss-crossing
piers. The main entrance is a double gateway, the

first being a high slim entrance with a Gothic arch.
The arch is under what would have been a
watchhouse of which only broken corbels and a
garderobe — on the left side of this outer entrance
projection — remain. The second entrance, about
two yards back from the first, is Roman arched.
This is flush with the outside walls behind those of
the outer entrance.

An impressive ruin from the village park
beneath, the castle does not disappoint the viewer
on the drawbridge: from here can be seen not
only the aforementioned double entrance but the
wide round corner tower to the left with a row of
rectangular, widely spaced windows (roughly the
height of the gatehouse garderobe) and arrow
loops (almost level with the drawbridge); the wall
to the left of the entrance, showing obvious signs
of bombardment; and the riot of gables and
chimney stalks which have survived the ruin of the
top storey. Some of the lower parts of the top
storey windows survive. These do not look so
dramatic from the park side.

Rising from long, spreading bases from the edge
of the rock, the three large towers were built of
dressed ashlar. The largest housed a polygonal
lord's hall which stood over the garrison post. This
was the south-west tower — originally lit by
narrow loop holes. (The garrison post is vaulted
like a dome and contains a harled fireplace,
decorated with dog-tooth mouldings of the 13th-
century Early English style.) A square tower
between this and another round tower completes
the set. A fourth interior tower once helped to
form an inner courtyard from which an outside
stair led to the first floor.

The east range has a very thick outer wall. Part of
its basement has been hollowed out of solid rock.
This highly vaulted basement contained the
bakery, with ovens and a well, and several large
vaulted cellars. Above the bakery is a vaulted
kitchen. This has roof ventilation, two large
fireplaces and a service room leading to the hall.
The hall was 72 feet long and 25 wide. There was
originally a minstrel's gallery at the south end over

49

wooden screens, the door and the fireplace at the north. Food was brought up to a pantry behind the screens by way of a stair leading down to a hatch in the bakery vault.

The lord's bedrooms were to the north of the east range. A stair linked the hall and cellars on one side, and a door on the other side led down to the prison. Underneath the prison is a dungeon, only reachable by a hatch. A window from which orders could be given overlooked the cellar. Above the hall would most likely have been additional bedrooms. There was possibly also a wing along the north side of the corridor, containing more living quarters.

Additions were made to Dirleton Castle during the 14th and 16th centuries. A Renaissance-style hall was built during the latter and a part of the three-storey building to which it belonged still stands — as do a 16th-century circular dovecot and a 17th-century bowling green.

Doune Castle

Stirling, Central

Historic Scotland, open to the public.

One of the most impressive of early Scottish castles to survive almost intact, Doune Castle stands on a raised site above the banks of the River Teith on the edge of the town of Doune. There is no exact date for its erection but ancient records show that it had been built as a royal palace in the reign of Robert III, therefore some time before his death in 1419.

Estate accounts show that Doune Castle was repaired in 1605, 1717, 1718 and in 1783, but by 1800 it had been completely unroofed and remained as a shell until it was restored in the latter part of the 19th century. Apparently the restoration was never completed.

The front structure is an almost rectangular tower with a semi-circular one joined to the front. It is five storeys high and had a garret, though now roofless. The lord lived in this tower and, therefore, it contained the hall, a suite of living rooms and a private chapel. The portcullis was controlled from this tower and it acted as a gatehouse. Entrance is through the arched doorway.

To the left of the gatehouse runs a wall 40 feet high and 7 feet thick. There is a parapet walk on the wall, with open rounds at the angles and semi-circular bartisans on corbels midway. On the south side is a low outer wall outside the great curtain.

On the opposite side of the west tower — which runs at right-angles to the hall and at right-angles from the great curtain — is an unusual building, quite difficult to describe. From the courtyard side it is quite pleasant to the eye. An outside walled stair over an archway and joined to the curtain wall leads up to an odd entrance on the first floor. A similar archway, at right-angles to the former, leads to the tower cellar. Coming to the other side of the tower, which is at right-angles to the hall, is another outside walled stair over a thinner arch-

51

way. This archway is at immediate right-angles to one of the same size on the ground floor. The stair is joined to the wall of the hall. (One of the arched hall entrances is at the foot of the stairway.) It leads up to another arched entrance on the tower, between the ground and first storeys. The stair wall-cum-banister stops to the left of the entrance at the corbel of a stairwell bartisan. The bartisan separates this part of the tower above the entrance from the remainder. There are several windows on the tower, large and small, both arched and square. (The hall windows are a similar mixture.) There are remains of gables on the top of the tower, showing it to have been double-roofed. The kitchen in this tower has a massive arched fireplace, an oven area, slop drains and a modern-looking hatch servery. Above the kitchen were sleeping quarters for either soldiers or servants.

This castle originally belonged to Regent Albany who governed Scotland during the minority of James I (1419–24). When James I had Albany executed in 1425 for an alleged implication in the death of his — the king's — brother, Doune Castle passed to the Crown. Prior to that it had often been the residence of royalty. It was garrisoned by a nephew of Rob Roy during the 1745 rising.

Drum Castle

Culter, Grampian

National Trust for Scotland, open to the public.

Set in pleasant woodland, the massive square, round-cornered tower of Drum Castle rises above the River Dee, 10 miles west of Aberdeen. It was built around 1286 to guard the lands on which it is sited, then a royal hunting preserve. It was one of the first medieval Scottish tower houses and is one of the oldest Scottish houses continually occupied by the same family.

The 75 feet high tower, with walls 12 feet thick at the base and tapering to 9 feet, looks superficially like a Norman keep. The parapet, with heightened open rounds, probably surrounded a garret at one point; now it is a stone-flagged floor.

The vaulted basement is entered via a mural stair on the first floor where there is also a barrel-vaulted hall. Corbels show that there had been an *entresol*. This very likely was the laird's bedroom as there are stone seats in the deeply set windows and there is also a garderobe. A newel stair is situated in the south-east angle but it would have been entered originally by a movable timber stair to the first floor, as with some other Scottish towers and many English ones.

A new *L*-shaped house, with dormer windows and crow-stepped gables, was added to the tower in 1619. This impressive Renaissance-style house was built by the prosperous 9th laird, Alexander Irvine. It has three storeys, and attics, with square towers on the outer angles and a circular, conically capped stair tower at the south-west. The servants' quarters were at ground level, with the great hall on the first floor reached by a straight stair, and by a small newel stair in the opposite corner, connecting the hall with the kitchen beneath. What were once the upper floor bedrooms are reached by several newels.

In 1876 David Bryce reconstructed the barmkin courtyard with an arched and gabled entrance to the north.

The hall of the tower was removed and made into a library. It was given new plaster-vaulted ceilings which bear the arms of families linked to the Irvines. The hall is now entered from the impressive Jacobean wing (where a vaulted stone-flagged passage runs the length of the basement). In what was once the hall of the 1619 building — and is now the drawing room — hang portraits by Raeburn, Reynolds and Gilbert. During the 1870s this part of the house was refitted with com-partmented timber ceilings and Jacobean chimney pieces to fit the fashion of the time.

Throughout the centuries the lairds of Drum played an active part in Scottish affairs. The original William, who was of the chiefly House of Bonshaw in Annandale, was armour bearer to Robert Bruce. He was given the castle, which was roughly 40 years old at the time, in the 1320s. (This gift was built by Alexander III. Irvine legend asserts that one Robert Cementarius was involved in building both the old Keep of Drum and the Brig o' Balgonie.) One died at the Battle of Harlaw in 1411. He was Alexander Irvine, Sir William's grandson, and the family would have been amply rewarded since victory was so important that the heirs of the fallen were awarded certain privileges. (Harlaw — a battle between Highlanders and Low-landers — was one of the bloodiest battles ever fought on Scottish soil. So blood-stained was the field that it is often referred to as 'Red Harlaw'.) The 7th laird, whose son was killed at the Battle of Pinkie in 1547—when the Scots were so badly routed and slain by the English that they called it 'Black Saturday'—was rewarded by James V for his actions against outlaws. They also played a notable part in the stirring affairs of the north-east, being greatly embroiled in feuding with the Forbeses and the Keiths.

The Irvines—originally spelt Irwin—were staunch supporters of the Stuarts during the troubled 17th century. The price of their loyalty was impoverishment and the sentence of death on the son of the 10th laird. Fortunately, the Restoration happened prior to his intended execution. They were not all warriors, however: the builder of the 17th-century addition was a patron of learning and donor of several bursaries to Marischal College, Aberdeen.

The castle is set in extensive gardens planted with many rare trees and shrubs, including a walled garden of old-fashioned roses.

Drumlanrig Castle

Dumfries and Galloway

Privately owned, open to the public.

Drumlanrig Castle, which stands in stately grounds high above the Nith Valley — about 3 miles north of Thornhill — is a three-storey high (four-storey at the corner towers), red-sandstone building. The basement floor is, however, on the ground, giving the building the appearance of being a storey higher.

The original castle was built by Sir James Douglas of Drumlanrig between 1513 and 1578. Very little is known of this structure other than that it was completely destroyed. The present castle was begun around 1645, to the design of Sir William Bruce, on the orders of the Duke of Queensberry. By the time the castle was completed, some 31 years later, the duke was so astounded by its cost that he refused to live in it! It is said that he actually lived there for one day. Though certainly a great deal older at its completion, one wonders if his grace was any wiser!

Though it is called a castle it is really a mansion. When it was built, fortalices were still considered to be necessary so it is, in a way, a link between the 'real' castle and its successor, the country house 'pretend' castle.

Drumlanrig is a great square built around four

sides of a courtyard. The result has been described as 'architectural excellence' — though its architect, James Smith, was perhaps too obsessed with order! Though very stately, the exactness of its symmetry from the outside gives it an air of austerity. The almost monotonous rows of box-paned windows are apt to remind one of a late 19th-century tenement block. The balustraded parapets, the tower roof corners' pepperpot turrets with ball-pointed, ogee-capped roofs, and the open-pedimented pillared entrance with its balconied central stair rescue it from blandness.

Externally, this building speaks more of power than of refinement — although it *is* refined. It is easy to imagine it serving as a school, hospital, museum or even as a hotel rather than as a private home.

It does not look so austere from the inner courtyard. The entrance there has a vaulted arcade supporting a terrace. The arcade is Renaissance in design but with a Gothic-style groined and ribbed vaulting. The open vaulted door porch is under a central tower. The door leads into a great entrance hall housing a handsome fireplace of a later period. There is an iron yett over the entrance doorway and another beneath it at the basement entrance.

Each angle of the court has projecting circular stair turrets, enclosing newels, with doorways decorated with fluted pilasters on Renaissance entablatures. The dates of construction are carved into window lintels showing the building's progress. The dates 1678, 1679 and 1689, carved on the north-east tower, show it to be the oldest.

There is further handsome Renaissance detail over the dining room doorway. The room itself has two fireplaces and a richly ornamented ceiling. Its four windows all face south. Immediately above this dining room is the drawing room — its walls being covered with tapestries — to the east of which is the main staircase.

At the south-east angle is a morning room with a plaster cast ceiling with heart-shaped panels. These panels no doubt allude to the heart of

57

Douglas heraldry—the Douglases being the castle's original owners. (The heart became part of their arms as they were the custodians of the encased heart of Robert Bruce; the Douglases carried it with them to the crusades.)

Architectural historians have in the past remarked that the north front of Drumlanrig bears a resemblance to William Bruce's design for Holyrood House's entrance. Though built to the design of William Bruce, as already mentioned, the architect was James Smith and one Lukup was the master of works. It has been reckoned by some that the real designer was Robert Mylne, Smith's father-in-law and the builder of Holyrood House. Now owned by the Buccleuch family, it houses paintings by da Vinci, Holbein, Rembrandt, Gainsborough, Reynolds and others. It is situated in excellent terraced landscape gardens.

Duart Castle

Isle of Mull, Argyll, Strathclyde

Privately owned, open to the public.

Standing high on a rocky peninsula jutting into the Sound of Mull, on the Isle of Mull, is Duart Castle. The earliest reference to this seat of the MacLean chiefs occurs in 1390 when the keep was built, probably by Lachlan Lubanach MacLean. However, the huge wall of the *enceinte* undoubtedly dates from the 13th century. Later additions were made in the 16th and 17th centuries. Hector Mor MacLean (who became the Duart chief after his predecessor was murdered in bed by the Thane of Cawdor for marooning the latter's sister on a dangerous rock with the intention of drowning her) extended the great tower — before he was kidnapped in 1540 by James V. The remains of Duart Castle were restored in 1912 by the architect Sir John Burnet for the then chief, Sir Fitzroy MacLean.

For most of its existence as an inhabited castle, Duart has been the possession of the somewhat romantic MacLeans — other than for a short time during the 17th-century civil wars when the Campbells took it. However, the Campbell chief, Argyll, bought up most of the MacLean debts at a later date and took over the castle.

The MacLeans claim to be descended from a 13th-century ancestor, Gillean of the Battleaxe (MacLean means 'Son of Gillean'. *Gill-Eathain*, in Gaelic, means 'Servant of John', and some of the more imaginative members of that great clan have understood this to mean that they are descended from a servant of John the Baptist!). Gillean's lineage has been traced through a Celtic abbot of Lismore and the royal house of Lorne, the ancient kings of Dalriada.

This was not the only Irish connection. Catherine MacLean, sister of the Duart chief, was a famous 16th-century MacLean. Her second husband was Calvah O'Donnell, ruler of Tirconail. But she was captured by Shane O'Neill, ruler of

Tyrone, who forced her to be his mistress. Both a Scottish dowager and an Irish queen, therefore, she had sons by both the O'Donnell and the O'Neill.

The length of the castle is 85 feet by 65 feet width; the walls are 6 to 10 feet thick and rise to 36 feet. There is a parapet and walk on top, pierced at a later date with gun loops. It is surrounded by a great windowless curtain wall, 30 feet high and 10 feet thick. Beyond the curtain wall is a deep fosse cut into the rock to give further protection. The entrance to the courtyard is in the south front, originally protected by a drawbridge over the ditch. The whole complex covers the rocky knoll on which it stands.

The three-storey tower had a ground floor cellar with a rock-cut well. Over the cellar was the hall. It was entered by the north-west wall at first floor level.

The south-east range was added about the middle of the 16th century, at a time when many other additions were made. The entrance gateway in the south-west wall was strengthened by the construction of a gatehouse and the upper parts of the keep were restored.

Throughout the civil wars of the 17th century, the MacLeans remained loyal to the Stuarts, taking part as staunch Jacobites in the risings of the 18th century. From that time the castle was allowed to decline into ruin by its Campbell owners, remaining so till 1912.

Duffus Castle

Moray, Grampian

Historic Scotland, open to the public.

Duffus Castle stands in grounds 5 miles north-west of Elgin. It was built in the 14th century but was preceded by a wooden structure with a palisade built on a Norman motte. This earlier castle was said to be one of the oldest in Scotland. Its bailey was raised above the surrounding plain for defensive reasons. It was still dominated by the mound — or motte — which could always be held if the bailey should be stormed and taken. The mound is surrounded by a water-filled moat.

Where the main gate would have led into the original bailey is now a massive gap in the curtain wall. Inside and to the left stand the remains of a small oven made of stone and clay. It is now protected by a glass roof. Ahead, the main tower of Duffus Castle rises from the summit of the motte. This keep was a fine structure in its day. It has a beautifully finished ashlar plinth and stands three storeys high, including the hall. It had timber floors spanning 36 feet.

The masonry of the hall is later than that of the keep, suggesting this part of the castle was rebuilt after the fire of 1452. About this time extensive works were done and a range of buildings along the north side of the bailey were added. (The curtain wall of the great bailey joined into the great tower after crossing the ditch, which has been long since filled in.) As already intimated, these are now in a ruinous state as is the tower. The latter shows some traces of burning and this may date from 1452 when Duffus was attacked by troops of the Earl of Moray. At its west end are two sunken cellars, beyond which is a detached building set in the slope of the motte. During the 17th century, a stair led up the back wall to the upper floors and battlements.

Following the cobbled causeway in front of the tower, the visitor will observe outlines of former domestic buildings set against the curtain wall.

Joist holes in the south and west sides show that several timber buildings once stood against it.

The original timber structure was the seat of the de Moravias, who later became the Murrays, the first owner being Freskin de Moravia. The estate passed to his son-in-law Richard Le Chen, a Plantagenet supporter. For his support of the English during the revolt against their domination, he received in 1305 a grant from Edward I of 200 oak trees. The purpose of these was for building his 'Manor of Dufhouse'. The grant was to compensate for the Scottish patriots burning the timber structure to the ground in reply to Le Chen's treason. It was overdue, however, for Sir Richard had started rebuilding a stone tower from 1300, giving it a stone curtain.

Soon after 1350 the last Cheyne, the lord of Duffus, died leaving an heiress, Mary. She therefore brought the barony to her husband, Nicholas, son of the 4th Earl of Sutherland.

The barony passed to Nicholas, who became the 4th Earl of Sutherland in the early 1350s. It remained in the family's hands till 1705 when it was sold to Sir Archibald Dunbar. He was an ancestor of the present owner, Sir Edward Dunbar.

Dunnottar Castle

Kincardine and Deeside

Historic Scotland, open to the public.

The spectacular ruined fortress of Dunnottar stands high on a promontory jutting into the North Sea, a mile south of Stonehaven. The dramatic promontory is almost an island surrounded by cliffs. The steep road to the castle descends to join the beach — itself under cliffs — at a natural bridge (or rising causeway) of rock.

A great tower was built around 1382 by Sir William Keith, Great Marischal of Scotland — at the cost of his excommunication by the Bishop of St Andrews. Sir William had the temerity to build on hallowed ground without permission. Fortunately, Pope Benedict XIII ordered his reinstatement on condition that the Great Marischal make suitable recompense for the use of the rock.

An older fortress must have stood there, near the church, for records mention that Wallace captured it from the English in 1296. The oldest part still standing, however, is the *L*-shaped keep. It stook four storeys high and the ruins of a gable show that it had a garret. The walls have gun loops and all angles have open rounds. Inside is a vaulted basement with domestic cellars and a small prison beneath the stairs. The first floor hall

was the common hall and the one on the second floor was the lord's hall. The common hall's original kitchen was in the wing until it was connected with a private room and the kitchen moved to the longest of the vaulted storerooms in the basement. The lord's hall had the usual withdrawing room — and other private rooms — attached.

Besides the addition of a massive gatehouse in 1575, a block had been built to the east of the keep earlier that century. Sometime during the 1500s a chapel had been built; and a west wing added around 1582. In the 17th century two wings were built to link up with the chapel.

It is obvious that there have been several periods of building as, from the main road (A92), the site looks more like a small village than an actual fortress.

There is a car park not far from the main road, but the castle is not nearly as inaccessible as it looks from there. Neither the beach nor the causeway can be seen from the road or from the car park, but a stroll will take the visitor down the steep descending path in a few minutes. The average person could walk from the causeway to the ruin in several minutes. It is well worth the effort — besides the fact that it is not as exhausting as one would think from the first viewing — because the spectacular ruin is even more impressive on closer inspection. A stroll over the summit of this lofty promontory will show the visitor more clearly that these buildings were never an integrated castle. The summit also affords a splendid prospect of the North Sea and the dramatic rolling coastline stretching to the northern and southern horizons.

The castle was to experience warfare during the Civil War. The 7th Earl Marischal, who had been an ally of Montrose in the capture of Aberdeen, found himself the latter's enemy when the marquis declared for the Royalists. On realizing that he could not win the Earl Marischal over to the Royalist cause, Montrose stormed Dunnottar. Though he could not dislodge the Presbyterians from the fortress, he compelled Earl Marischal to 'stand on his own battlements and see the fires of war devouring his broad acres'.

Charles II was entertained at Dunnottar in 1651 and the castle was besieged by the English in the following year, until May 1652. One of the darkest moments in its history was in 1685 when 122 men and 45 women (Covenanters) were imprisoned in the 'Whigs' Vault', a room 54 feet by 15 feet, where many of them died.

During Dundee's campaign, 17 suspected Jacobites from Aberdeen — including a professor of mathematics — were imprisoned there for over a year. In 1715, Dunnottar was in Jacobite hands and, in 1718, the 10th Earl Marischal's lands were forfeited and the castle dismantled.

Dunnottar regained the appearance at least of its roofs in 1990 when it was used to represent Elsinore in Zefirelli's film version of *Hamlet*.

Dunvegan Castle

Isle of Skye, Highland

Privately owned, open to the public.

Dunvegan Castle stands overlooking Loch Dunvegan on the north-west side of the Isle of Skye. It claims to be the oldest inhabited castle in Britain and is lived in by the family of its first owners, the MacLeods. Dunvegan has been their home since 1200. Though parts of the castle are reported to date from the 9th century, the massive square tower to the north-east — the oldest part — shows signs of construction work dating from the 15th to 19th centuries.

The flagpole tower is a 16th-century decoration to which was added, in the same century, a wing known as the 'Fairy Tower'.

Some of Dunvegan's walls are 10 feet thick and it houses a 15th-century dungeon. Its treasures include relics of Bonnie Prince Charlie, Rory Mor's two-handed sword, a drinking horn presented by the 16th laird and the 'fairy flag' reputed to have been captured from the Saracens during a crusade. Legend has it that this flag has magical powers: if waved, it will bring victory to the MacLeods — which has happened twice; if spread on the marriage bed, it ensures children; and if

unfurled, herrings will come to the loch in countless shoals. The Macleods have always taken its powers seriously; the flag may to this day be used only in emergencies. Apparently, this was the condition the fairies demanded before presenting the gift. Coinneach Odhar, a 16th-century seer, predicted that the flag would be unfurled for the third and last time causing MacLeod power to depart and much of their land be sold. Proof of the prophecy, Odhar claimed, would be through Norman—fourth of the name—perishing in an accident and a vixen giving birth to cubs in a turret. Norman MacLeod was blown up on HMS Charlotte and his pet vixen had cubs in the west turret. These and the rest of the prophecy were fulfilled after the flag was accidentally unfurled by the chief's business manager. He did not know of the legend or the prophecy.

Visitors have included James V, Boswell accompanying Johnson, and Sir Walter Scott.

Edinburgh Castle

Edinburgh, Midlothian

Historic Scotland, open to the public.

In the centre of Scotland, and almost in the very heart of Midlothian, stands Scotland's premier castle. It towers above the city on a cliff of basalt rock—an extinct volcano—443 feet above sea level. It is awe-inspiring from whichever part of the city centre it is viewed.

There may have been fortifications on the rocks from earliest times, probably from the Iron Age. Indeed, the original name of the town, Dun Edin, is claimed to be derived from Dun Eadwine—the fortress of Edwin. The only reliable information available is that Malcolm III, Canmore, and his queen, Margaret, made it their royal residence during the 11th century.

We can only imagine what the fortress looked like then as nothing remains of it now. Some believe that the buildings may have stood on the higher part of the rock. The chapel, which Queen Margaret had built for herself, still stands. It is most certainly the oldest Roman Catholic chapel in Scotland and was restored in 1853. The stained-glass windows portray St Andrew, St Ninian, St Columba, St Margaret and William Wallace.

The castle is entered by a drawbridge over the old, deep moat. In niches on either side of the gateway stand bronze statues of Bruce and Wallace. The pathway behind the gateway is cut through solid rock and leads to the portcullis gate. This features some Renaissance work and is said to have been defended by two portcullises. The upper section dates from 1886.

Above the portcullis gate is the State Prison, also known as Argyll's or the Constable's Tower. It is part of the defensive works erected by David II about 1358 and dismantled in 1573. The walls are 10 to 15 feet thick. The tower is named after the two Argylls, father and son, marquis and earl, who were in turn imprisoned in the castle prior to their executions for adherence to the Covenant. The earl was confined in the cell immediately above the archway, while his son's incarceration was in a vault below the great hall. Montrose, the Principal Carstaires, and many others were imprisoned in the Argyll Tower.

On the left a flight of steep stairs ascends to the citadel. The road to the top passes the Argyll Battery on the edge of the cliff overlooking West Princes Street Gardens. From the parapet walks there is an incredible view over the north of Edinburgh across the Forth to the Fife hills. Looking eastwards, one can see over the buildings on the north-east side of Princes Street to the Forth estuary and the North Sea, the horizon broken only by the top of the Scott monument and the Calton Hill summit.

Carrying on towards the citadel we arrive at the Governor's House and the former armory on the right and a couple of other buildings. On the brink of the precipice is the old Sally Port—through which the body of Queen Margaret was stealthily carried away by her confessor, Turgot. Here, the historic interview between Graham of Claverhouse and the Duke of Gordon took place; after Claverhouse had climbed up the face of the rock in the hope of persuading the duke to join him in raising the Highlands against William of Orange.

Passing through the 'Foog's Gate' one reaches

the citadel, otherwise known as the King's Bastion, and the Bomb Battery—the site of Malcolm Canmore's Palace or Hunting Seat.

The first object of note is Mons Meg, a monster cannon. An inscription on the carriage states that the gun was made at Mons in 1486. It was taken to the Tower of London in 1754 and returned to Edinburgh Castle in 1829. Its length is 12 feet, calibre 19.5 inches, and weight 5 tons.

The aforementioned St Margaret's Chapel adjoins the battery.

On the Half Moon Battery (dating from 1574), the eastern front of the citadel, are a beacon basket and the well. The latter is cut through rock to a depth of over 100 feet.

On the summit of the castle stands the War Memorial, consisting of a gallery of honour. It replaced the barracks. The palace yard (overlooked by the Memorial) contains nearly all the historic apartments of the castle. Queen Mary's bedroom, at the south-east corner, was the birthplace of James VI (and, later, I of England). A number of portraits and other early relics can be seen in these confined apartments.

The vaulted Crown Room adjoining the royal apartments contain the Scottish Crown Jewels or 'Honours Three', the crown, sceptre and sword of state. The crown was refashioned for James VI, the sceptre presented to him by Pope Alexander VI and the sword by Pope Julius II.

The castle is an experience which no visitor to Edinburgh should miss.

Edzell Castle

Angus, Tayside

Historic Scotland, open to the public.

The ruined castle of Edzell, 7 miles north of
Brechin in the foothills of the Grampians, occupies a strategic position. This ancient seat of the
Lindsays, earls of Crawford, is an early 16th-
century keep, later enlarged into a country
mansion. In 1604, a larger garden was added as
was an ornamental wall. The wall has designs of
boxed chessboard-like niches under carved star
shapes, alternating—between thin pilasters—
with large, single, box-like niches that look like
they were originally arched but have slab lintels
inserted to break the arch. These box niches are
under relief carvings in pointed ovals, repre-
senting the liberal arts, celestial deities and the
cardinal virtues. Based on designs that Lord
Lindsay acquired in Germany, they are under
arched and pedimented niches that look similar to
dormer windows. Apparently, they were built to
accommodate busts.

The *L*-plan tower at the south-west angle of the
main courtyard replaced an older castle. This was a
Norman castle, and was the seat of the Stirlings of

Glenesk. It passed to the Lindsays through marriage, in 1357, to Catherine Stirling. The tower is four storeys high with a garret inside the wallhead gable.

The late-16th-century addition, erected by David, 9th Earl of Crawford, consisted of a three-storey *L*-shaped range. It had gabled roofs — without parapets — to the east and north of the keep.

Edzell Castle was never completed. The north side buildings extend only half way along the courtyard and, on the south side, there are foundations for rooms which may never have been completed.

The summerhouse is a self-contained, oblong, two-storey building. It has its own stair tower, gun loops and angle turret. The window pediments are handsomely carved and the moulded doorway in the front of the stair tower has been superseded by a modern entrance. There are two vaulted basement rooms, one of which is ribbed. The bath-house tower at the south angle contains a stone sink.

Edzell has had a peaceful history. Though fortified it never sustained siege but was garrisoned for a while by Cromwell's troops in 1651–2. It *was* vandalized after the 1745 rising though not in warfare. Apparently the vandals were unpaid creditors wreaking their vengeance on the stones of the castle's walls!

The Lindsays sold Edzell in 1715 to pay off huge debts. It is now in state care.

Eilean Donan Castle

Ross and Cromarty, Highland

Privately owned, open to the public.

This picturesque and, certainly, one of the most photographed of Scottish castles takes its name from the island on which it stands: Eilean Donan. The island—which in turn is named after its first recorded resident, the Celtic saint Donan—stands at the mouth of Loch Duich, opposite Skye, where it meets lochs Alsh and Long. It is connected to the mainland by a bridge.

The original part of the existing castle was built in 1220 by Alexander II as a stronghold against the Danes. Later that century Alexander III gave it to Colin Fitzgerald, a son of the Irish Earl of Desmond, and ancestor of the MacKenzies. Fitzgerald had helped Alexander to defeat the Norwegians at the Battle of Largs. In 1331, the Earl of Moray decorated the castle walls with the heads of 16 MacKenzies, his host's men, after executing them for law breaking.

The castle was captured by the Earl of Huntly in 1504, and escaped capture in 1579 when the assailant, Donal Gorm, was struck in the foot by a stray arrow. This chance incident resulted in his bleeding to death and the subsequent departure of his dispirited men. The castle was less for-

tunate, though, in 1719 when William MacKenzie, the Earl of Seaforth, had it garrisoned with Spanish troops during the Jacobite rising. Three English ships bombarded it to ruin. The Spanish allies of James must have felt betrayed by the Scots. Only some of Lochiel's Camerons, MacGregors under Rob Roy, some Atholl men and MacKenzies bothered to fight with them. Most Jacobite Highlanders drifted away.

It remained in a ruined state till 1932 when it was restored and extensively reconstructed. It serves as the seat of the MacRaes and shelters the Clan MacRae War Museum.

The three-storey keep was built in the late-14th century when Eilean Donan was in the hands of the Earl of Ross. It has a gabled garret, open rounds and a projecting missile device (though not above the modern entrance). It served as a look-out, a point of refuge and a secure and comfortable residence. Originally, it had a stone-vaulted basement without outside access and was entered by a wooden staircase from above. Its present vaulting is largely 20th century. The banqueting hall—where the great hall of the Ross keep had stood—is now full of historical knick-knacks and fine furniture.

The dramatic scenery is a perfect backdrop to this spectacular castle.

Elcho Castle

Perth and Kinross, Tayside

Historic Scotland, open to the public.

Elcho Castle stands on the south bank of the Tay, about four miles east of Perth, looking across the river to the rolling Sidlaw Hills. This somewhat mournful ruin of whinstone rubble — with quoins and freestone facings — occupies a position on Moncrieff Hill. The site is reputed to have been a favourite hiding-place of William Wallace, presumably in an earlier castle that stood there or nearby. Sadly, some of its history is hazy as early records do not survive. One story claims that when in hiding there as a fugitive, Wallace slew a comrade whose fidelity he doubted. The following night, when staying at Goskhall, the man's ghost is said to have tormented him.

The Wemyss family were first in control of the lands in 1468. It was to become an earldom in 1683 when Sir John Wemyss was created 1st earl at the coronation of Charles I. It was forfeited, however, after Culloden as Lord Elcho had taken Prince Charlie's side in the 1745 rising. He not only sided with the prince but he survived Culloden and escaped to France. The castle's last mention in historical records was in 1773 when, during a

famine, a violent mob from Perth attacked it as it was being used as a grain store.

Elcho Castle is, in plan, a long oblong block with a square stair tower at the south-west corner. Three other towers project on the north side facing the Tay, two of which are round stair towers with corbels squared at the top into look-out posts. The other contains small apartments. A large angle turret projects out of the roof at the south-east corner.

The square tower has a crow-step gable on the southern side and open rounds at the parapets' angles. The entrance is in the re-entrant angle, giving access to a turnpike with steps 7 feet wide. In the kitchen on the ground floor is a fireplace which is almost the size of the wall it occupies in this small room. Its flu is a feature of the north front roofscape.

Relics of fine plasterwork can still be seen in the hall on the first floor. From there, three stairways lead up to bedroom accommodation with private lobbies and garderobes. The original wrought-iron grilles still protect the castle's windows.

Elcho Castle, in decay by the 1780s and reroofed in 1830, still belongs to the Earl of Wemyss and March.

Falkland Palace

Near Kirkcaldy, Fife

National Trust for Scotland, open to the public.

Falkland Palace is in a fortunate position for attracting sightseers. It stands in the main street of the picturesque market town of Falkland, a royal burgh since 1458, which retains the size and atmosphere of a village.

The palace looks austere when viewed from the High Street side. This is due to a combination of grill-barred windows, a fortified roof and, on the west side, the massive two-towered gatehouse — which, were it not for the ornate painted carvings, would look like a prison entrance. The east side of the facade is something like a square tower built of coarse rubble.

Once through the gatehouse entrance visitors find themselves in the lawn-covered courtyard where the walls contrast elegantly with those seen from the street. Though reminiscent of the Elizabethan period, they are French Renaissance, built during the reign of James V. The windows are

in bays divided by slim butresses, modelled as piers made to look like classical columns. Each bay is also decorated with a pair of sculpted medallions.

At right angles to this (south) range of the palace is the east range, joined to it by a turnpike. Though not a ruin, it is apparent that it is of similar design to the south range. It is said to have been burnt by accident by Cromwell's soldiers.

At the back of the gatehouse entrance, steps lead up to the entrance hall. It has more the feel of a study than a hall. The wall lamps which illuminate the carved furniture and panelled walls give it a warm glow. From here, visitors ascend via a turnpike to the keeper's bedroom on the second floor. The bedroom itself leads into the adjacent dressing room. The door dividing the rooms displays a carved panel bearing the portrait of the 3rd Marquis of Bute. It was this Lord Bute who in the 1890s was responsible for the extensive restorations to the palace.

The bedroom is dominated by an ornately carved and inlaid bed, originally from Rossie Priory in Perthshire. On the walls are massive portraits (copies) of Charles I, his queen Henrietta Maria, and Charles II; they are on loan from Holyrood House.

Descending to the drawing room on the first floor one is aware of the liveable atmosphere—the portraits of earlier Stuart monarchs adorning the walls notwithstanding! Perhaps this is due to the warm colours of the decor as well as the small sizes of the rooms. Falkland Palace is still lived in by the family of the present keeper, Ninian Crichton Stuart.

A door in the east wall leads into the chapel where mass is celebrated each Sunday by the local Roman Catholic community. On its north wall are Flemish tapestries depicting Joseph and Benjamin. Its other salient features are a finely painted panelled ceiling, the crucifix above the altar and a 'Madonna and Child' statue.

Running the length of the chapel's north side is the tapestry gallery which leads up another turnpike to the library on the second floor. It is more like a Victorian drawing room than a palace library (except for the elaborately painted ceiling with *trompe-l'œil* decoration), as the countless pictures and ornaments create a cluttered look.

The next place visited is the bakehouse at the foot of the turnpike. The stone-flagged floor and the stone vaulted ceiling have changed little since the 16th century.

From there the visitor ascends to the terrace of the roofless east range and to the king's room. Though not the original king's bedroom, it does give the impression of a late-16th-century palace interior. Over the fireplace are emblazoned the royal arms of Scotland of James V's day and colourful panels adorn the ceiling, as do friezes the walls. The room contains the so-called 'Golden Bed of Brahan', dating back to the time of James VI. A door leads into the original lavatory.

Another turnpike leads up to the 'Queen's Room', though its real identity is questionable as the queen's apartments have never been satisfactorily identified. The main exhibits here are the exact copy of a bed from Darnick Tower, Melrose, and the copy of Archbishop Sharp's cabinet. From the shuttered windows are views of the town, the garden (where MacDuff's original castle stood), and the tennis court.

The tennis court is the oldest in Britain. Situated in the stately gardens, it was built for James V in 1539. All courts today are derived from two French types, the *jeu à dedans* and the *jeu quaure*. Falkland's is the world's only *jeu quaure* court. The austere stone walls and the seatless penthouses remind one more of a dungeon than a tennis court.

There are conflicting tales of a palace ghost.

Glamis Castle

By Forfar, Angus, Tayside

Privately owned, open to the public.

Glamis Castle is an impressive sight when approached from its long, grass-banked, tree-lined avenue. The main gates, which are in the village of Glamis — 5 miles from Forfar — lead into the avenue.

The first impression is of extreme complexity. It is, however, an L-shaped plan tower house with added lower wings with round towers at their furthest angles. There is also a later circular tower at the re-entrant angle. This, unusually, contains the main entrance (though not to the public). On the inner corners of the lower wings are circular corbelled pepperpot turrets with larger ones on the visible four corners of the tower house. The latter rise above the crenellated circular tower. There is a circular, capped dormer window between the inner corner of the left side of the tower and the central circular one. Above each of the outer facing walls of the L-tower are two gazebos sitting on a balustrade of peculiar design. Two chimney pieces either side of the circular tower (which reach to the same height as the caps of the pepperpot turrets) and a roof tower with a dome-like pointed roof between them, add to this impression of complexity. So does an extra wing added to the lower eastern range. The 17th-

century present castle was built in the French chateau style.

The almost fairy-tale look of this red sandstone building has encouraged its critics. One stated that it is like something out of Disneyland. Walter Scott called the 18th-century remodelling an 'atrocity'.

Glamis has a delightful wood-panelled chapel, each panel—on the walls and low ceiling—containing a painting of either a saint or a Biblical scene. These are by the Dutch artist Jacob Witt, who was brought to Scotland to decorate Holyroodhouse.

Near the back entrance is a pend leading to the castle museum. Inside the right of the pend is an antique shop where visitors can purchase limited reproductions of some of the castle's Georgian furniture.

The castle is stocked with treasures including weaponry, splendid tapestries, paintings and a collection of Meissen porcelain. The billiard room houses tapestries depicting Old Testament stories and the great painting *The Fruit Market* by Rubens and Snyders. Another of its treasures is the Old Chevalier's sword, inscribed with the words 'God save James VIII, prosperitie to Scotland and No Union'.

A 21-foot high Baroque sundial stands in the front gardens. Over to its right is a nature trail leading to the tranquil Italian garden. The latter includes an attractive fountain, two stone gazebos with seats, an archway of trees, herbaceous borders and two wrought-iron gates made by local blacksmith George Sturrock. These were commissioned to commemorate the Queen Mother's eightieth birthday.

As well as being the Queen Mother's birthplace, her daughter, Princess Margaret, was born at Glamis. Their relatives, the Earl and Countess of Strathmore and Kinghorne, still live in a wing of the castle. There is a hidden crypt where the 1st Lyon of Glamis and the 4th Earl of Crawford used to play cards. It is claimed that they both did so on Sundays with the devil. Though only a legend, uncanny things did happen in the vault, ceasing only when it was sealed up.

The chapel is said to be haunted by Lady Glamis who died after being terribly tortured. Odd, considering she died more than 150 years before it was built! Nor was Macbeth the Thane of Glamis. That was merely an invention of Shakespeare. It is another mere legend that claims Duncan was murdered there (in the oldest part of the castle called Duncan's Hall) by Macbeth. Duncan is known to have been slain in Morayshire, apart from which, the vault was built at a later date. It is however quite likely that Duncan hunted in the area — though there is no proof either way — and it is just as likely that a hunting lodge stood on the site. The first castle was erected on this same valley bottom — convenient for huntsmen — rather than in a more defensible position on the surrounding slopes.

Hermitage Castle

Roxburgh, Borders

Historic Scotland, open to the public.

Hermitage Castle, from the outside, seems to be an apt structure for its bleak, windswept Borders surroundings. Its exterior is a grimly austere, rubble-built pile of sheer walls, sloping slightly to its now roofless parapet. The parapet runs the length of its plan—a kind of squat *H*-shape with one of the *H* uprights trailing slightly longer than the other. Understandably, this dour-looking structure, with its appropriate wild and remote Liddesdale environs, gave birth to the story of its original owner, the wicked Lord Saulis. Legend tells us that due to his excesses enraged locals had him boiled in lead. Reputedly, this happened at the stone circle of 'Nine Stane Rig' a mile or so away from the castle. The authority for this story is merely a ballad by a minor 18th-century poet. The legend goes on to say that 'unable to support the iniquity within its walls' the castle partly sank beneath the ground.

The grimness of the building is exaggerated further by the smallness of the windows, the wide, splayed 16th-century gun loops and the identical, massive, gaping arch entrances on the east and

west faces. More at home on the gateway to an oriental town, they are quite incongruous on a Scottish castle. The archway on the east side has a garderobe to its left and is directly under a crow-step gable. There are similar gables to the north and south ends of the same wing, at distant right-angles to the central one. The archway at the opposite end of the castle is to the left of centre. This is the trailing part of the *H*-plan's upright.

Perhaps there was reason behind the grim exterior. The wild Borders weather would have demanded sheer walls and small windows — as would have the wild Borders people! These precautions would have helped to make Hermitage Castle more resistant to their attacks. As Liddesdale was 'England's western way into Scotland', a castle well prepared for such an eventuality was essential. As if the structure were not sufficient, artificial ditches and banks were joined at an early date to gullies of two streams to make a moat. The moat seems somewhat superfluous, however, as it would not have offered serious obstruction to an enemy.

One of the most impressive — and oppressive — looking medieval castles in Scotland, Hermitage is thought to have been built between 1338 and 1365 as a manor house of the Dacres; possibly built on the site of a 13th-century castle. Oblong in plan, this 'manor house' consisted of a central court enclosed by east and west cross wings and by screen walls on the north and south. The north screen contained a turnpike rising to the first floor and the south contained the entrance. The only part of this structure remaining is the lower part of the walls facing the courtyard.

The castle was reconstructed in 1388 and in 1400 an oblong wing was added to the south-west corner. By this time Hermitage Castle had risen to four storeys.

The massive tower house of several building periods has figured in many episodes of Scottish history and was held for a time by Bothwell. The original structure — prior to the Dacre's manor house — was an early 13th-century rectangular enclosure of stone walls three feet thick, ten feet thick on the north wall where the newel stair was enclosed. This was a domestic structure though the aforementioned moat may date back to that time, explaining its seeming superfluousness.

A castle on the site is recorded as having been repaired towards the end of the 13th century by order of Edward I. It appears to have changed hands several times in the early decades of the 14th century. Its form was quite different then as only the original tower would have existed. The first additional work—making it three times its original width—did not occur until the late 14th century (prior to the *H* uprights being added).

It was captured in 1338 by Sir William Douglas of Liddesdale from the English baron Ralph Neville, who had received it from Edward III. It was granted later that century to William, 1st Earl of Douglas.

Inside are pleasant arched doorways in coursed ashlar.

The castle, belonging to the Scotts of Buccleuch, is now in care as an ancient monument.

Palace of Holyroodhouse

Edinburgh, Midlothian

Crown owned, under the care of Historic Scotland, open to the public.

At the opposite end of the Royal Mile from Edinburgh Castle—and a good 400 feet beneath it—sits the Palace of Holyroodhouse. Sitting under the 823-feet-high Arthur's Seat, it seems, from the forecourt, to be more of a mountain fortress than a royal palace on the edge of the centre of a metropolis. Though it does look more like a baronial mansion than an actual castle, it has enough towers and crenellations for it to fall into the category of castle!

Above the entrance gate to the forecourt is an impressive display of wrought-iron scrollwork. The centrepiece contains a stag's head with the Holy Rood (cross) between its antlers. This reflects the legendary encounter of David I with the stag while out hunting and his consequent inspiration to start building the abbey in 1128. Once through the gates, the visitor must walk to the left of the palace (northwards) to discover the oldest part— the abbey ruins.

The abbey was the result of a charter David gave to the Benedictine canons. It was dedicated to the Holy Rood from which the palace takes its name. It is also believed by some to have taken its name from the famous Black Cross that Princess Margaret (Canmore's queen) is said to have brought to Edinburgh. This was a black castket, in the shape of a cross, reputed to have held a relic of the cross on which Christ was crucified.

The abbey had luxurious apartments which eventually became a royal residence. It was when James IV lived here that he began building the palace including the northern tower and other parts, containing those that were to become Queen Mary's apartments. In 1543, both the abbey and the palace were burned by the English, only the church and north-west tower escaping.

After being rebuilt to become the residence of

Mary and her son, James VI, it was burnt again in 1650 but the greater portion of the edifice survived. Eight years later Cromwell ordered the palace to be restored. This restoration was pulled down in 1671 when Charles II decided on the erection of a new palace. Bonny Prince Charlie held court at Holyroodhouse in September–October 1745, before setting off on his ill-fated march on London. In 1830–2 Charles X of France lived there in exile. Edward VII, as a boy, spent some time in the palace while studying under the rector of the high school.

On entering, after turning to the left, one comes to the Picture Gallery, the largest apartment in the palace — 150 feet long, 24 feet wide and 20 feet high. During his brief stay in Edinburgh in 1745, Prince Charlie held balls and concerts there. Since the Union, the Gallery has been used for the election of representative peers of Scotland and the levees of the Lord High Commissioner to the General Assembly of the Church of Scotland. Here hang portraits of more than 100 Scottish kings from Fergus I to James VII. They were executed by the Flemish artist Jacob de Witt who was contracted to paint them within two years. Obviously, they were from de Witt's own imagination, and many of the portraits have very similar features.

From the gallery the next important room *en route* is the Duchess of Hamilton's and then Lord Darnley's apartments in the old tower of the palace. Darnley's rooms consisted of an audience chamber, the room called Lord Darnley's bedroom and his dressing room. In these rooms hang many portraits and fine specimens of ancient tapestry.

A door in the audience chamber leads to a staircase by which Queen Mary's apartments are reached. There is also a small private staircase (closed to the public) that the murderers of Rizzio used to gain access to the queen's rooms. The first room of the suite is Mary's audience chamber, 24 feet by 22 feet. The panelled ceiling contains arms and monograms of various royals. There is an oratory at the east end and a portion of frieze from Mary's time still adorns the walls.

Mary's bedroom is a little smaller than the chamber just mentioned. The ceiling also has panels adorned by emblems and initials of Scottish sovereigns. The walls are hung with tapestries depicting the fall of Phaethon. Several of Mary's relics are to be seen, including examples of her needlework. Adjoining the bedroom is a small dressing room, hung with decayed tapestry. This is in the eastern turret of the tower. A little to the left of it is a door communicating with a secret staircase on the north side of the room. Near the head of this staircase is another door leading to the most interesting of Mary's apartments: the Supper Room in the west turret. It was here that Rizzio was attacked by Ruthven and a mob of conspirators, including Darnley, to be dragged through the bedroom and audience chamber to the head of the principal staircase where they stabbed him to death. A brass plate in the floor marks the spot.

A handsome staircase in the south-west angle of the quadrangle leads to the modernized state apartments on the first floor. The Throne Room, drawing rooms, and other rooms, contain fine paintings, tapestry, furniture, panelling and ceilings.

The Chapel Royal ruins are entered from the north-west of the quadrangle; the walls and nave of which are the only portion of the old abbey church still standing.

In the garden, on the north side of the palace, is a sundial called Queen Mary's dial but it refers to Henrietta Maria, queen of Charles I.

At the outer edge of an enclosure of trees stands a late-16th-century building with a conical roof and dormer windows. It is known as Queen Mary's Bath due to a legend that she bathed there in wine. In 1789, during roof repairs there, a jewelled dagger was found stuck in the sacking.

Huntingtower Castle

Perth, Tayside

Historic Scotland, open to the public.

On the outskirts of Perth, where the A9 meets the A85 and near to the River Almond, is Huntingtower Castle. This highly impressive mixture of two medieval tower houses, joined by a gangway at parapet level, was probably built in the early 15th century as a gate tower, and later modified to become a more conventional tower. A plain, *L*-shaped tower with an extra storey was added later that century by the first Lord Ruthven. However, it was not joined to the earlier tower, though a wooden bridge was added to link the battlements. There may have been some defensive purpose in this arrangement. The space between the towers was known as the 'Maiden's Leap'. Its name comes from the story of a Ruthven daughter who, in order to escape discovery in her lover's bedchamber, leapt the distance between the parapets. Apparently, wishing her never to repeat the feat, her lover married her!

Though the battlements are ruins, parts of them can be walked over safely. Indeed, some particularly ruinous parts have been reinforced with metal rails. They are worth scaling as they

offer pleasant views over the surrounding countryside.

In the 17th century, another building was added, the steep roof of which reaches to the rim of the parapet of the eastern tower and declines to between the third and fourth storeys of the western tower. This early example of 'infill' between two towers is especially pleasing to the eye on the north side. In fact, this north side is more interesting architecturally. The 'infill' protrudes a little northwards from the eastern tower but is flush with the northward part of the western tower — as the back of the furthest west part is about the same distance southwards as the back of the eastern tower. The eastern tower has an arched doorway in this side and the northmost part of the west tower has a double-walled stairway leading up to the first floor. A large inverted V on the face of this part of the tower shows that a lower roof — and therefore another building — was once joined to the tower here. This would mean this entrance did not exist at the time or was approached by wooden stairs.

Until 1600, Huntingtower was known as Ruthven Castle and belonged to the Lothian family of that name who had been in Perthshire since the 12th century. The 3rd Lord Ruthven was one of the assassins of Rizzio. It is thought that the purpose of the murder was to shock the pregnant queen into a miscarriage. Unfortunately for Ruthven's son — who was beheaded by James VI — it failed! This son, the Earl of Gowrie, was involved in the so-called Raid of Ruthven in 1582. This was when the earl invited the king, then aged 16, to the castle for a hunting holiday. While there, Gowrie and several other nobles forcibly demanded the dismissal of the royal favourites the Duke of Lennox and the Earl of Arran. The king, being under an unspoken but nevertheless forced imprisonment, reluctantly complied for a time. Unfortunately for Gowrie, the young king escaped. He at first forgave his captors but changed his mind three years later and ordered Gowrie to be banished. The earl only got as far as

Dundee before being arrested and sent to Stirling, where he was beheaded on 4 May 1585.

James also falsely accused Ruthven's two grand-sons—the following Earl of Gowrie and his brother, Alexander Ruthven—of attempted assassination and had them killed on the spot. James perhaps feared that they might wish to avenge their father and so acted quite unscrupulously. While visiting Gowrie House—the Ruthven Perth residence—James ran to the window of its tower and screamed that he was being attacked. Proof was later unearthed that this was a sham in order to have the earl and his younger brother murdered. James's men far outnumbered the Ruthvens' for one thing. He had both men dispatched without further ado. The two bodies were sent to Edinburgh where they were hanged, drawn and quartered at the Mercat Cross. James then ordered the name of Ruthven to be abolished and he changed the name of the estate to Huntingtower. The citizens of Perth were outraged.

Huntingtower contains some very fine painted wooden ceilings of c.1540, with ornamental knotwork patterns, thought to be the earliest Scottish tempera-painted ceilings in existence. It is now in the care of Historic Scotland.

Huntly Castle

Huntly, Aberdeen, Grampian

Historic Scotland, open to the public.

The ruins of Huntly Castle, sometimes called Strathbogie, stand high above the nearby rocky gorge of the River Deveron and its junction with the Bogie. The castle stands just above Huntly, the town famous till recently for its hosiery manufacture and wool dyeing.

The original castle, Strathbogie, was a timber structure built in the 11th century by the Celtic rulers of the area. The first Norman baron to settle there was Duncan, Earl of Fife, in the 12th century. He either restored the original structure or built another; either way, the result was a motte and bailey surrounded by a deep, wide ditch. The interim buildings were earth and timber and this fortress stood till 1452 when Douglas, Earl of Moray, burned it to the ground.

The 1st Earl of Huntly was created in 1436 and he began building the next castle in 1454. This keep

92

was partially destroyed in 1594 but much of the stone structure remained. The elaborate top storey, its crowning glory, dates from 1492.

The lower storeys are coarse rubble while the upper is of dressed freestone, displaying on the south side three handsome oriels, alternating with flush rectangular windows. The oriels are half-hexagon in plan. An inscribed frieze runs the length of the wall over the window tops and a parallel one runs beneath them, thus over the corbelled oriels' balconies. On the south side of the south-west tower is another oriel. This has a smooth face, making a neat contrast with the coarse rubble of the tower's top storey. This oriel is also half-hexagon in plan. The corbel under its balcony comes almost to a point, like an inverted pyramid. Its top rises to the rim of the roofless tower—where there was once a parapet—decorated with a staggered corbel that runs over the half-hexagon protuberance. Two chimney pieces and, between them, the pediment and lintels of a dormer window still stand. So does the pentagonal cap-house through which one descended into the attic. The basement of this tower held prisoners of the 'Cock o' the North' (the 6th earl).

The north-east tower has a fine doorway with a huge armorial panel above, dating from 1602. In the room above the hall a fireplace from 1606 has survived to indicate the Renaissance character of the interior.

James VI's men had inflicted serious damage on Huntly, only for it to be restored once again. But due to the Marquis's loyalty to Charles I, the Cromwellians destroyed the restoration. Since then, Huntly has remained a ruin, albeit a fairly substantial and impressive one. It is now an ancient monument.

Inveraray Castle

Argyll, Strathclyde

Privately owned, open to the public.

Set in the glorious scenery of Argyllshire, Inveraray Castle is quite incongruous. This odd-looking castle would look out of place in any setting, though, as it looks more like a hotchpotch of buildings than an actual castle. The steepled towers on the four corners, with their crenellated parapets, are the nearest thing to castle architecture on the whole building. The crenellations sit above Victorian Gothic windows with intersecting tracery—giving the building the air of a Methodist chapel! As the towers also have Gothic-style windows, they seem to be at variance with the windows on the ground floor and first storey. These are Georgian style under Gothic arches, which are again different from the dormer windows in the roof! The latter appear to be mock Elizabethan with triangular pediments. The Georgian main door has an ogee Gothic-style porch—as if to further state that the designer (Roger Morris, assisted by William Adam and his sons John and Robert) was having fun rather than producing a serious work of architecture.

On a wet day, the grey stone slabs of which Inveraray is constructed turn black. As the main entrance is on the gloomy, northern side, it can on such a day seem to be a dark, sinister place. As this is the seat of a clan with one of the most notorious histories in Scotland, some would say it is an apt home for them! However, on a sunny day the southern side can appear quite pleasant.

There is something quite liveable—even homely—about Inveraray. Perhaps it is due to the lack of fortifications and also to its compact size—more that of a country squire's manor than the seat of a duke. The gardens too appear to have been built more for pleasure than to flaunt power. The main path to the castle's entrance is fairly unassuming, planted either side with various bushes, as is the entrance itself. About half a dozen steps take you into the castle. There is no magnificent portal or balustrade. So, in spite of its initial dourness, from closer up it is inviting and pleasantly eccentric. So much for Campbell notoriety; Inveraray is the antithesis of a symbol of exploitation or exclusivity.

When the castle was being built in 1743, the 62-year-old duke who had newly inherited the estate rehoused his tenants from their sordid dwellings into comfortable houses. He saw to it that the town of Inveraray was rebuilt with Classical-style public buildings—more attractive than the castle, some maintain. The townsfolk also prospered from the Duke's patronage as well as from his encouragement of tourism.

Once inside, the visitor is further reminded of Inveraray's homeliness. The Tapestry Drawing Room, with its famous Gainsborough above the fireplace, and the dining room, with its huge mirrors and impressive wall and ceiling decoration, as two examples, emit a lived-in feel. However, a MacDonald could easily feel unnerved on entering the Armory Hall as the walls from floor to high ceiling are a morbid display of guns, swords and battleaxes!

The Campbells have occupied Argyll from time immemorial. Historians reckon that it cannot be ascertained if they are descended from the Scotti from Ireland who settled in the area in the 6th century or whether they are of aboriginal British or Pictish origin. If they were either of the latter, it would help explain why they warred for centuries with their neighbours the MacDonalds, MacDougals, MacGregors and MacLeans, etc, who were of Gaelic Irish origin. Interestingly, they are the only Highland clan to possess a mythical surname; the rest have patronymics. They are known as Clan Diarmid in Gaelic, supposedly descended from the Ossianic hero Diarmid. It may be that being menaced by the colonizing Scots they adopted their Gaelic language and folk legends.

The resilient Campbells tended to prevail over their enemies. Innischonnaill Castle on an island on Loch Awe was their headquarters in the Middle Ages. The 1st Earl of Argyll was created in 1457 and he built the *L*-shaped tower at Inveraray on the banks of Loch Fyne. It was Duke Archibald who saw the present Inveraray Castle completed, though neither Morris nor his assistant Adam lived to see it.

The drawing room is one of the most important rooms in the castle. It contains larch wood cabinets covered by tops of marble quarried in Glen Tilt, a full-length portrait of the 4th Duke (above one of these cabinets), and a bust of him — sculpted by Lawrence MacDonald — in an alcove at the end of the room.

Dr Johnson and Boswell visited the place, though the Duchess snubbed Boswell and fussed over Johnson. Keats and Burns, respectively, stayed at a nearby inn.

Kellie Castle

Pittenweem, Fife

National Trust for Scotland, open to the public.

Not to be confused with Kelly Castle by Arbroath, Kellie Castle, 3 miles north of St Monans, is one of the masterpieces of Scottish baronial style. Its situation is particularly fortunate for those visiting the area for the first time. Kellie is fairly near to Pittenweem, St Monans and Elie, the most picturesque fishing towns on the south-east Fife coast. It is almost *T*-shaped in plan, with the crossbar of the *T* running from north to south and the ascender part running from west to east.

The earliest part of Kellie Castle was the north tower, built around 1360. The east tower was built in the 16th century; 1583 is carved in one of its walls. During the following century the main block was added, joining the towers together. Soon after, a southern tower was added. This is about a storey higher than the main block and almost the same height as the north and south towers.

The entire ground floor is vaulted. An impressive square stair rises from the main doorway at the front of the south tower to the first floor. This is where the hall — 50 feet by 20 feet — is situated. Four different turnpikes lead to the apartments above the hall.

The 17th-century exterior of this pleasant and almost quaint castle remains virtually complete and unspoilt. Even its great square-domed ceiling survived 19th-century dereliction. Fortunately, Professor James Lorimer leased the ruinous castle in 1878 and proceeded to restore it. His foresight and enthusiasm saved this handsome relic of an older and more proud Scotland. His son, the famous architect Sir Robert Lorimer (who spent much of his boyhood at Kellie), was responsible for part of the garden layout and also for the design of an ogee-roofed gazebo. The gardens include lawns and well-maintained roses.

An earlier castle belonging to the Sewards stood on the site. The present structure was built by the

Oliphants, who owned the lands from 1360 to 1613. As the 5th Lord Oliphant squandered his inheritance he sold Kellie to Sir Thomas Erskine, a favourite of James VI, who was involved in the Gowrie murder (*see* Huntingtower).

Worth seeing are the 17th-century plaster ceilings and the withdrawing room's painted panels.

Sir Robert Lorimer's son sold the castle in 1970 to the National Trust for Scotland.

Kildrummy Castle

Aberdeen, Grampian

Historic Scotland, open to the public.

The 'noblest of northern castles' stands in undu-
lating ground 1.5 miles south of the village of the
same name. Kildrummy Castle, an imposing ruin
on the summit of the ridge above the north side of
the main road to Strathdon, is guarded on both
sides by a ridge.

The first castle, probably a timber structure, is
mentioned in Barbour's *The Brus*. It tells of how
the castle was burnt by a traitor 'Osbourn to
name'. The Norman lords built another of earth
and timber in the 13th century and then a stone
one later that century. It resembled Bothwell
Castle and, so, resembled the Chateau de Coucy,
near Laon, on which it was based.

The castle was besieged in 1306 by Prince
Edward of Caernarvon (later Edward II) who
captured and dismantled it. It was restored again
by 1333 by which time a new gatehouse and two
massive drum towers had been added — only for it
to be besieged two years later by the Earl of Atholl.
It was in the hands of the Wolf of Badenoch,
bastard son of Sir Alexander Stewart, from 1361 to
1367. David II captured the castle in 1367 and in
1404. Sir Alexander Douglas — the castle's owner
at that time — was murdered by assassins hired by
the Wolf's son, Alexander Stewart. Two years
later, Stewart took the castle, forcing the Douglas
widow to marry him so that he could acquire the
earldom of Mar.

James IV bestowed the Kildrummy estate on the
1st Lord Elphinstone in 1507. His family held it until
1626 when the legitimate heirs, the Erskines, Earls
of Mar, forced them to return it.

In 1654, Cromwell captured Kildrummy and
burnt it. It was captured again in 1690 by
Claverhouse's troops — who once more set fire to
it to prevent it from falling into the hands of
William of Orange. After the Earl of Mar's abortive
rising in 1715, the castle was dismantled, to remain

a local quarry till 1898. That year Colonel James Ogston organized excavation and restoration work on the site. In 1951, his niece, Mrs Yates placed the castle in the care of the state.

Though now a ruin it is a substantial indication of the plan — as almost all of the lower parts of the walls remain to show the original (11th-century) outline. A great shell of the north-eastwards tower still stands — most of the inner side now gone — as does a great deal of the square tower next to the base of the northwards-western tower. (Kildrummy's plan is like a great *D* with the straight side facing northward but the north-west side tilted slightly southwards; thus its tower there is termed 'northwards-western'.)

The standing ruin shows how remarkably symmetrical and uniform in layout the castle was. In the middle of the semi-circle of the *D* — the south-east — is the ruin of what was once a twin cylindrical-towered gatehouse. At either side of the gatehouse, halfway between where the walls of the semi-circular plan meet its straight (northwards) wall, are the ruins of two other *D*-plan towers, the bevelled walls facing outwards. The only part of the plan's symmetry being slightly aggected is through the northwards-western tower. It is much wider than the north-eastwards tower and is not so evenly balanced on its angle.

Kildrummy stands with its northwards side to a steep tree-filled gorge. It is protected on the other sides by a deep and wide dry moat. This was probably dug as a defensive measure for the castle's builders.

The quarry beneath Kildrummy has been converted into a superb rock garden.

Linlithgow Palace

Linlithgow, Lothian

Historic Scotland, open to the public.

Linlithgow Palace is perhaps best known as the birthplace of Mary, Queen of Scots. Her father, James V, was also born there. In fact, the palace's connection with the House of Stuart continued till after the 'Glorious Revolution' of 1688–9 which was to remove her descendant James VII and II from the throne.

This grand ruin has the very feel of history about it. Though a manor house probably existed on the same site — roughly mid-way between Edinburgh and Stirling — from the time of David I, who founded the burgh in the mid-12th century, the earliest records date the castle from 1301.

Edward II spent some time there in 1310. It did not return to Scottish hands till 1314, soon after Bruce had defeated Edward at Bannockburn. The English retook it after Cromwell defeated the Scots army at Dunbar in 1650. It is not difficult for the visitor to see why it would be an important army stronghold. It is an ideal site for a military base.

The palace is approached through the southern gate. Directly above the arch, and immediately under the battlements, are carved painted arms of the four orders of chivalry to which James V

belonged. Through the gate St Michael's church stands to the visitor's right, built between 1424 and 1535. In lieu of a spire it displays (in the opinion of this author) an incongruous and particularly ugly contraption, reminiscent of 'futuristic' sculpture, which can be seen for miles from the surrounding countryside. The palace is straight ahead.

It is entered through the south gate, built by James V around 1535, which leads into the central court. The centrepiece is an elaborately carved three-tiered, octagonal fountain, c.1538, reminiscent of Linlithgow's Mercat Cross. A veritable work of art, its lower tier is divided equally by ornate Gothic-type flying butresses, the lower ends of which are alternating pillars with sculpted designs: four slightly higher and slightly more ornate than the other four. These butress pillars, each separated by quatrefoil stone screens, reach the pedestals of baroque-looking figures on the second tier. There is a smaller version of the quatrefoil screens between each. Above the heads of the figures are gargoyle-type faces on the base of the third tier. This base holds up four pillars which themselves support a massive crown.

One's first impression is of pleasant surprise as each inner facade is from a different building period. On the east is the great hall and original entrance of James I; on the west the state apartments built by James III and IV; on the north the 'New Work' constructed for James VI; and, looking back to the south, the English-looking transe of James IV and Margaret Tudor. Each corner has a turnpike and the north range has one in the centre.

These extensive architectural additions made by each of the Jameses (except for James II), from between 1424 and 1624, add to its feel of history. (James II was apparently more of a military turn of mind than an aesthetic one, unlike his namesakes. Those military interests left him little time for improving Linlithgow and caused his premature death.) However, the exterior is as aesthetically pleasing as the interior. The east front of the palace displays the impressive gateway of James I.

This open archway is under a great carving of royal arms, with a large shield under a crest and mantling, and two smaller shields either side. Just under this heraldic carving are two slender niches, crowned and corbelled, either side of the arch.

Though the original four-towered barbican is long gone, part of its wall still stands; as do three impressive arched butresses making bridges to the barbican wall ruin. The face of this side of the castle is covered haphazardly with several types and sizes of windows.

From under the north range on the banks of Linlithgow Loch, the towering facade, with its more orderly rows of windows, is the most stately side.

Linlithgow Palace is impressive from any approach. As it is built on a hill offering splendid views from across the loch, a walk around the castle means going up and down braes. It is worth the effort. It is equally impressive at night-time when floodlighting makes it look even more dramatic.

Loch Leven Castle

Loch Leven, Perth and Kinross

Historic Scotland, open to the public.

The rugged ruins of Loch Leven Castle stand on an island to the west of the loch and can be seen clearly from the M90 as it bypasses Kinross.

A small but substantial ruin still remains, this being an early-15th-century keep set into a barmkin — the north and east sides at right-angles and the other two multi-angular. In the corner almost opposite the keep is a small circular tower with gun loops. There have been other buildings within the barmkin — as a gable-end and window show on approach — including a hall and a kitchen range. The date of this fine, early specimen of a Scottish tower house is suggested by the absence of wall chambers, the scarcity of stairs, and the unusual height of the main entrance on the second floor. But, as this type continued to be built, an early date cannot always be inferred.

The five-storey oblong keep is constructed of square rubble and is five feet thick in parts. It tapers in a few inches above the first floor up to the parapet where it comes out again to match, approximately, the width of the ground and first floors. The parapet has corbelled rounds — perhaps originally bartisans — on three of the angles. The top of the parapet walls — like those of the rounds — are long since gone. It is difficult to say whether they were roofed, though most likely they were. The parapet has an unusual kind of corbelling. It is difficult to ascertain from ground level if it is a type of staggered corbelling or, instead, machicolation. Perhaps it was corbelling merely designed to give that effect to a potential assailant. The parapet also has windows to light the top floor. It may even at one point have been gabled.

There are various sizes and shapes of window looking into the courtyard side where there is also a squared doorway in the centre. This is slightly below the surrounding ground level of the courtyard. The original entrance, a hooded arch, was by a movable staircase to the second floor above the basement on the east side. This led to the hall, which has a fireplace and stone window-seats. The room above the hall has four windows, the one to the east having been an oratory with altar-shelf and piscina. Beneath the hall, and entered from above by a turnpike, are the vaulted kitchens. These kitchens — on the first floor — have a fireplace, salt-box, sink and drained wall-closet. At basement level, and also vaulted, is another room with a trap door from the kitchen. From here is the present main entrance to the tower.

The most famous historical figure connected with Loch Leven Castle was Mary, Queen of Scots. She was imprisoned there by Protestant lords on 17 June 1567, to escape the following year in romantic and dramatic fashion; a boy rowed her to the shore where some horsemen took her to an army of waiting Hamilton supporters. It was not, however, Mary's first visit to the castle. She had been there two years earlier, but then voluntarily, when she had an interview with John Knox. Apparently, it was quite amicable and she presented the fiery reformer with a watch as a goodwill gesture.

The castle had been a royal residence since 1257 when Alexander III and his young queen were taken there, forcibly, from Stirling. The English besieged it in 1301 till Sir John Comyn recaptured it.

Noltland Castle

Pierowall, Orkney

Historic Scotland, not open to the public.

Noltland is one of the two largest Z-plan castles in Scotland; Drochil in Peeblesshire being the other. It is on the island of Westray (in north-west Orkney, about 24 miles as the crow flies from Kirkwall) where it overlooks the harbour of Pierowall.

It was built during the last quarter of the 16th century, reportedly incorporating sections of an earlier structure built for Bishop de Tulloch. It was seized by Sir Gilbert Balfour of Mountquhannie, brother-in-law of the Bishop of Orkney. (Sir Gilbert is best known for his involvement in the murder of Cardinal Beaton at St Andrews in 1546.) This was during the time following the Reformation when church lands were being 'redistributed' to impoverished lairds, providing them with funds for building. Sir Gilbert probably built the present structure. He designed many of the additions to Noltland and turned it into a personal hide-out — hence the heavy fortifications. The 4 feet thick walls with numerous tiers of gun loops (71 gun loops can still be seen on the surviving ruin) were much needed. Sir Gilbert's family were embroiled in most of the intrigues of the reign of Mary, Queen of Scots and he personally had to flee to Sweden where he was subsequently executed.

A dripstone which runs much of the length of the castle — running from window to window on several of the wall faces — give the impression of dividing the fortress into two neat halves, upper and lower. Except for those parts where the broken gables, machicolations and turret corbels can still be seen, the upper half looks like a plain tenement building while the lower half — in stark contrast — is nothing but a hotchpotch of gun-loops. As these are different sizes and do not fit into any pattern, they make the bottom half of the castle look quite ugly. They would have made those quarters very cold in the winter-time, and also extremely gloomy, as they lacked windows.

Furnished with corbelled parapets and cylindrical turrets and topped with a high-pitched roof, Noltland Castle looks quite forbidding on its bleak outpost. The roofless northern tower and what remains of the link section of the roofless main block both rise to the full height. Both the northern tower and connecting wall have a projecting parapet. Perhaps Sir Gilbert had to flee before he was able to raise the castle to its intended four storeys; it may never have been finished.

A southern extension was added in the 17th century and additional work in the 18th century extended the ranges to the east and west.

The main door to Noltland is in the south-west tower and, inside, a guardroom or prison sits under a spiral staircase that leads to a vaulted chamber. The chamber leads into the great hall. From a landing, a smaller stair ascends to the upper storey, formerly living rooms and the original hall. Wall ruins with an arched doorway stand in the south courtyard.

Soon after the defeat of Montrose, the castle fell into ruin.

Rothesay Castle

Isle of Bute, Strathclyde

Historic Scotland, open to the public.

Rothesay Castle, in the county town of the same name on the Isle of Bute, is one of the most remarkable in Scotland. The original castle was an enormous keep built around 1098, first recorded when attacked by the Norsemen in 1230. It survived the attack and it is believed that its towers were added after the siege. The Pigeon Tower in the north-west still survives from that time in good condition — though practically the whole of its donjon on the east side was rebuilt in the 19th century.

The castle is a great circular curtain, strengthened with four massive round towers. It stands on a flat-topped mound surrounded by a water moat. The upper part of the wall once had a bretasche — a defensive wooden boarding — as the putlog holes still remain.

Rothesay Castle is unusual in that the parapets have been built into later masonry. It is as if later builders tried to seal them up — albeit unsuccessfully, for they are still visible. It is one of the only 13th-century castles to still show these parapets. Interestingly, they show that the loopholes in

Rothesay were specially designed so that an archer could keep a look out while reloading his crossbow in shelter.

Inside the donjon are the porter's lodge on the left and the guardroom, and on the right a postern leading to the moat. A trap door in the entrance floor opens into a damp prison. Further along this passageway are slots for a portcullis and steps nearby lead to the courtyard. In the courtyard stands the two-storey chapel of St Michael, built of whinstone rubble, possibly 16th century. Behind the chapel an outside stair called the 'Bloody Stair' leads to the summit of the curtain wall.

The great oblong keep to the north was added by James IV and James V to combine the functions of a gatehouse and a royal residence. Traces of ribbed vaulting suggest the royal apartments included an oratory. The tower had four storeys. The garret and crow-step gable—containing a chimney head—still stand. Its walls contain chutes to the moat from latrines in the upper floor. The castle is entered through this tower via a bridge from the main road over the moat.

The noble family of Bute had been made the hereditary keepers of Rothesay Castle in 1498, but the Earl of Lennox captured it in 1544 for the English, expelling the Butes. In the 17th century it was held first for Charles I and then for Cromwell. When the Roundheads withdrew in 1659, they partially destroyed the building. What remained was set on fire by Argyll's Highlanders during the 1685 rebellion. It remained much in the condition they left it until 1816–17 when it was repaired.

St Andrews Castle

St Andrews, Fife

Historic Scotland, open to the public.

About a 5-minute walk from the medieval walls of St Andrews Cathedral, and less from St Salvador's Chapel, stand the ruins of a once enormously powerful castle. St Andrews Castle is on a rocky cliff directly above a bay beach facing out to the North Sea. Founded in 1200 by Bishop Roger, it was a castle of *enceinte* enclosing a pentagonal courtyard with a tower at each corner and buildings all round. It was cut off from the town by a deep dry moat, presently spanned by a wooden bridge.

The south front is the best-preserved section, consisting of a keep-like tower with a battered base and chequered corbelling under the parapet, cannon-spout water chutes, and bases of land-ward-facing angle turrets. The original entrance — the outline of which remains — was through the lowest storey over the moat. This entrance (in the south front) adjoins the tower. There is a Renaissance gateway — mid-16th century — with vaulted guardrooms to either side. Flanking this entrance facade at the south-western end was a circular donjon-like tower. Most of it has been demolished, however.

Very little remains of the great hall on the east side and little more than the ruins of the vaulted cellars of the kitchen tower in the north-east

corner have survived the ravages of time and the weather. The north-west tower contained two vaulted rooms, one level with the courtyard and one lower. The lower room was also the entrance to the still surviving bottle dungeon, hewn out of the rock. Its narrow neck made escape almost impossible; however, the castle's most distinguished prisoner, the poet Gavin Douglas, Bishop of Dunkeld, did manage to get out of it alive. It is reputed to be one of the worst dungeons in the world.

St Andrews Castle has had a chequered history. It was 'completely demolished' after a three-week siege during the Wars of Independence when Sir Andrew Murray routed the English garrison. From that time (1336) it lay ruined for more than half a century.

Cardinal Beaton lived there, in shameless luxury, and it was here he was assassinated by a group of Protestants while spending the night with his concubine.

After the castle (occupied by Protestant infiltrators) fell in 1547 to the Catholic troops of Mary of Guise, Beaton's successor, Archbishop Hamilton, had it patched up, adding the front range to the west of the fore tower.

Stirling Castle

Stirling, Central

Historic Scotland, open to the public.

On looking up from the A91 dual-carriageway at
Stirling Castle, perched up on the massive face of
basaltic rock, it is not hard to share the thrill that
Burns undoubtedly felt when he wrote 'Here
Stuarts once in Glory Reigned'. The castle looks
thrilling; understandably so, when considered
that it occupies what must be the most powerful
and strategic position of any Scottish castle
except, perhaps, for Edinburgh. Indeed, it is
similar to Edinburgh Castle in situation and
design.

It forms the link between Highlands and Lowlands, which is why it has been called the 'Key to
Scotland'. The poet Alexander Smith stated,
'Stirling, like a huge brooch, clasps Highlands and
Lowlands together'. Another wrote that whoever
holds 'Stirling and its bridges splits Scotland in
two'. Therefore, prior to the Scots seeing themselves as a united people, Stirling was an important defensive site.

Records show that a castle existed before the
11th century. This was a timber structure. The
present castle is not the same one that overlooked
Bannockburn on that fateful day of 25 June 1314,
when the Scots inflicted the most humiliating
defeat an English army had ever experienced.
Soon after the victory, Robert Bruce had the castle
dismantled. Nothing of the castle of his day
remains. The earliest structures still to be seen
date from the reign of Robert II. He was Bruce's
son-in-law and first of the Stuart kings.

Perhaps more than any other castle, Stirling
represented Scotland's military resistance to
English aggression in the Middle Ages. During the
Wars of Independence it was constantly attacked,
its buildings destroyed only to be rebuilt. Edward I
of England seized it in 1296; Wallace recovered it,
with many others, a year later. The following year
the English retook it only to lose it to the Scots

once again the next year. This time they held it for another five years till the year of the Great Seige (1394) which lasted for three months. The English were then to hold it for ten years — till Bannockburn.

Records of 1381 refer to the North Gate, a rear entrance at the north end of the rock, known as the Nether Bailey. The modern road to it still passes beneath this arch. But the North Gate was an addition to an existing castle. In 1373, Robert II's son, Robert, Earl of Menteith and Fife, was made keeper. He held the post till 1424 when James I returned from captivity in England.

Most of what remains of Stirling Castle dates from the 15th century. It was probably James III who built the central turreted gatehouse, curtain walls and flanking towers which give the castle its impregnable and proud air. He also had the great hall built to hold parliaments and state ceremonies. James IV carried on in his father's footsteps by adding to the castle. He erected a new palace behind the previous building. His son, James V, in turn continued and completed the work on the royal palace. This is a remarkable Renaissance building constructed under the direction of Sir James Hamilton. It was possibly designed by Thomas French; Robert Robertson the carver was responsible for the woodwork. Recessed panels alternate with grilled windows. The upper half of the panels are arched and contain sculptures on slim columns. The sculptures, some complete and some mutilated, are both grotesque and beautiful. The palace has three arched entrances, one under the central grilled window and the others, respectively, under each end grilled window. There are crow-stepped gables at either end but facing in towards the courtyard. Each apex supports a royal animal sitting on a bowl-like, four-legged pedestal.

This architectural masterpiece heralded the end of the Middle Ages and it stands adjacent to another triumph of Renaissance architecture — one of the earliest in the British Isles — the palace of James V. James's wife, Mary of Lorraine, must

have been responsible for the defences in front of
the forework known as the Spur, now either built
over or incorporated into later developments.
This spur is similar to the Italian-designed spur at
Edinburgh.

James VI built the chapel in 1594, reputedly after
demolishing the one erected by James V—in
which his mother was crowned and he was later
baptized. Its facade is still very much in its original
condition, except for the removal of coats of arms
and badges put there in Cromwell's time. It was
given a Classical entrance in the form of a
triumphal arch, with three pairs of windows along
the walls on either hand. The gable-end windows
are a Roman-arched pair, leaving one to wonder,
as they are chapel windows, if they represent the
tablets of the Decalogue—a common feature in
Jewish synagogues. The painted decoration was
by Valentine Jenkins.

A vaulted passage leads from the chapel's west
end to the garden. The room above the passage is
supposed to be where James II, assisted by Sir
Patrick Grey, murdered Earl Douglas. This cannot
be so: the room was not built when the murder
occurred.

Around the castle are two very old gardens and
underlying the castle rock to the west stood what
was once the King's Park. It was enclosed by a high
wall and contained the famous Knot Garden, built
in 1627. Other buildings within the castle precincts
include 'Mar's Wark', which is the ruin of a
16th-century town house, and the Argyll Lodging,
a 17th-century mansion.

Tantallon Castle
North Berwick, East Lothian
Historic Scotland, open to the public.

A ruin as rough in outline as the rugged rocky cliffs on which it stands, the dark red mass of Tantallon Castle looks out from the East Lothian coastline to Bass Rock and the North Sea beyond. It also commands spectacular views over land, ranging from the Lammermuirs to the Lomonds.

Though the rough outline of the castle blends in with the coastline, it consists of a crenellated curtain of dressed ashlar, 50 feet high and 12 feet thick. This frontal wall is flanked by towers, one round and one a *D*-shaped plan. A massive rectangular gatehouse keep juts out of the centre section of the curtain. Reminiscent of 14th-century French chateaux, it is 80 feet high and has four storeys for living accommodation above the portcullis chamber.

The gatehouse keep was the defensive centre, the chamber above the entrance passage being used as a fighting deck as well as for working the drawbridge and portcullis. The entrance was strengthened further by inner gates that folded shut against the court.

The aforementioned living quarters above the portcullis chamber included the lord's hall and, two storeys higher, his private rooms. There were additional though somewhat cramped sleeping quarters in the rooms of the tall frontal turrets of the tower.

Described by Hugh Miller as being 'three sides of a wall-like rock and one side of a rock-like wall', it is one of the most impressive of Scotland's castles. Hermitage and Bothwell are perhaps the only two castles in more awesomely striking settings. Its impregnable air begat a local proverb of the impossible: 'It's as easy to knock down Tantallon as build a bridge to Bass Rock.' It also inspired Scott's description in *Marmion*:

> And sudden, close before them showered
> His towers, Tantallon vast;

Broad, massive, high and stretching far,
And held impregnable in war,
On a projecting rock they rose,
And round three sides the ocean flows.
The forth did battled walls enclose
    And double mound and fosse;
By narrow drawbridge, ôutwards strong,
Through studded gates, an entrance long,
    To the main court they cross.
It was a wide and stately square;
Around were lodgings fit and fair,
    And towers of various form
Which on the coast projected far,
And broke its lines quadrangular,
Here was square keep, there turrets high,
Or pinnacle that sought the sky,
Whence oft the warder could descry
    The gathering ocean-storm.

A castle had existed on this site since before 1300, known as 'Dentaloune', the property of the Earls of Fife. It was the last medieval castle of *enceinte* to be built in Scotland. The 3rd earl, James, was commanded in January 1446 to forfeit his lands for leading a rebellion against the Crown. When he died a few months later, James II granted the castle and lands to Earl James's brother, George. George's son, Archibald, succeeded him in 1463 as the 5th earl. James IV ordered him to ward himself in Tantallon for joining a treasonable contract. He defied the royal order and three months later, in October 1492, the king laid siege to Tantallon.

Douglas held Tantallon till 1639 when Covenanters took it over. Monk attacked and captured it in 1651. A Douglas, the Earl of Angus, returned to take it soon after. In 1699, the castle and barony were sold to Sir Hew Dalrymple, Lord President of the Court of Session, who abandoned the building and left it to decay. It is now in the care of Historic Scotland.

Threave Castle

Dumfries and Galloway

National Trust for Scotland and under guardianship of Historic Scotland, open to the public.

Though a ruin, the dour and impregnable-looking Threave Castle, which occupies a low grassy island on the River Dee, still stands defiantly. Though the roof and the parapets are gone, this massive oblong keep of five storeys still looks as if it could repel another siege.

When it was originally built it had a garret and was flanked by two drum towers, of which two storeys of one remain. This is linked by the ruin of the curtain wall to the stump of the other.

Between these ruins stands an impressive gateway entrance, rising to about the height of the two-storey tower, which is reached by a wooden bridge. The gatehouse led via a movable wooden bridge to the entrance at *entresol* level. Through the entrance was the kitchen—which was the upper section of a high-vaulted basement—containing a fireplace and a stone sink in the window embrasure. The room beneath may have served as another kitchen as it also contains a sink, a well and a drain. In the north-west corner is a trap door leading to a deep dungeon.

A wheel stair rises to the great hall, with a garderobe in an angle and a fireplace. Originally

there was an outside entrance to this room. It was reached from a wooden bridge spanning to the gatehouse parapet.

The castle, rising to a height of 70 feet, with walls 8 feet thick, was built by Archibald, 3rd Earl of Douglas and Lord of Galloway. It was built around 1370 to control Galloway for David II and it has been remarked that this grim building did little to help the earl's sinister reputation. His contemporaries called him 'Black Archibald the Grim'. Being considered dour, harsh and uncompromising, though, would have been an asset for the Earl of Douglas, especially as he was bound to impose his will on a lawless region where murder and pillage were the norm. Thus it would have been for practical reasons rather than from a lack of aesthetic taste that he ordered his craftsmen to erect a tower which in appearance was as grim as its master.

The odd thing about Threave Castle — especially as it was built as if to flaunt impregnability — is that Black Archibald made no provision against gunfire. This is quite an oversight considering soldiers from the British Isles had met with cannon 25 years before the castle's completion. Eighty years later, Earl William added defences to rectify this weakness.

The Covenanters besieged Threave Castle in the 17th century and it has been a ruin since. By Charles II's time, the nobility required more luxurious dwellings.

Tolquhon Castle

Tarves, Aberdeen, Grampian

Historic Scotland, open to the public.

Tolquhon was the principal manor house in the ancient thanage of Formarture. It is situated about 2 miles south of Tarves and 15 miles north of Aberdeen.

The original structure, a small but strong rectangular tower, was built in the 14th century by the Prestons of Craigmillar, near Edinburgh. It passed to the Forbeses in 1420 when Marjorie Preston married Sir John Forbes. What survives is a castle of two main building periods: late 15th century and 1584–9.

Sir John built what is probably the oldest part of the castle still standing, the Preston Tower. It remained unaltered until 1584 when the 7th laird, William Forbes, employed the architect Thomas Leiper to build a large quadrangular mansion on to the tower. Mansions were unusual for Aberdeenshire, where tower houses were the norm. The tower became the north-east angle of the

courtyard, but this once-parapeted keep is now largely collapsed. It is still crowned by a fragment of machicolated parapet and the vaulted basement and part of the great hall on the first floor still survive.

The rest of the castle survives to the wallhead. It is constructed of rough rubble, the steps on the crow-stepped gables being the only parts that are cut ashlar. This gives the gables a quoined-like appearance. All the 16th-century buildings are on record as being roofed in 1838 but the roof had collapsed before 1887, by which time much of the structure was rapidly deteriorating.

There is a remarkable gatehouse with two drum towers with heavily grated windows. (Each houses a ground floor guardroom.) The wall between them, roughly the same width as each tower, is decorated with armorial carvings and French Renaissance-style sculpture. These are in the form of two tablets, one directly above the other, almost immediately above the narrow arched doorway. The gatehouse, like the rest of the adjoining buildings, is unroofed.

Unusually, Tolquhon combines a wide variety of gun loops and shot holes (four of which are on the gatehouse alone) and has courtyard windows, large for the period. There is much evidence of a high level of domestic planning in its design.

Visitors enter through an arched doorway in the south courtyard. Approached from the courtyard, it gives access to a vaulted passage in the main block. This passage leads to three vaulted cellars and the kitchen. The latter houses a large fireplace, stone sink and a hatch. Stairs link the kitchen and the wine cellar to the hall and to the laird's room above. Beneath the kitchen level was a prison.

The castle was deserted by the end of the 18th century and it is now an ancient monument.

Urquhart Castle

Drumnadrochit, Inverness

Historic Scotland, open to the public.

Urquhart Castle stands high on a sandstone promontory projecting from the western shore into Loch Ness. It commands sweeping views up and down the loch — almost as far as Inverness to the north and Fort Augustus to the south — hence its use by 'monster spotters'.

As the ruins occupy a site well below the level of the road, they would have been vulnerable to attack from above. The stronghold would have been entirely at the mercy of catapults or archers. However, it was probably built with the concept that attack was to be expected from the loch, from which side the defences were excellent.

This area had been used as a fortress since Pictish times and it seems that it was inhabited when St Columba visited the Great Glen (Glenmore) in the 6th century.

A castle stood at Urquhart in the 12th century. Very little is known about it, other than that it was a motte and bailey — but unusual in that it had two baileys and the natural rock was its motte. The earliest surviving remains are of the 13th-century castle built by Alan Durward, the 1st Lord Urquhart. A massive thick-walled keep, in which he and his family resided, dominated the upper bailey, along the loch-side wall. Only its outlines

remain. A chapel once stood on the mound to the west.

The gatehouse and the 16th-century residential tower are the least ruinous. It is believed that the gatehouse was erected in 1296 on the orders of Edward I after he had taken Urquhart. A conflicting theory maintains that the gatehouse — consisting of two drum-fronted towers backing on to a square blockhouse — is a much later structure; Edwardian castles were much more grand. The entrance passage was defended by iron-strapped wooden doors, portcullis and 'murder holes' in the ceiling — appendages through which the occupiers could fire or drop missiles on an army powerful enough to have advanced that far. The tower on the left looks as if it has been bombed relentlessly! It was deliberately blown up with gunpowder in the 1690s by a retreating garrison. The damage was immense.

The base of the partially-collapsed tower at the northern end of the castle is the oldest part, dating from the 13th century. The bulk of the interior, including stairways, fireplaces and privies, is 16th-century work. The small square corner turrets must have been comfortable as each was furnished with a fireplace, window and personal privy.

Urquhart Castle was taken over by the powerful Comyns in 1252, due to Durward fleeing to England after being accused of treason. Edward III was unsuccessful in trying to bring it once more under English rule. It last saw action in 1689, when it repelled a Jacobite assault.

Architectural Terms

angle The inner or outer corner of a building.

apex The highest point of an architectural or masonic feature (often triangular).

architrave The lowest part of a lintel over a doorway or of an entablature above pillars.

ashlar Properly, building stone in the condition in which it arrives from the quarry: squared but not finished. Dressed ashlar is that which has been cut to smoothed sides.

bailey A castle courtyard or ward: area of ground enclosed by a wall on which the castle's domestic buildings stood.

barbican Outwork defending the entrance to a castle.

Baronial Type of mock Gothic, particularly Scottish.

Baroque 17th- and part 18th-century style characterized by exuberant decoration and expansive curvaceous forms.

bartisan A roofed turret on the upper angles of a castle.

bretasche The covered wooden platform surrounding the top storey of a keep, used by soldiers for dropping missiles. It was replaced by machicolation.

buttress A stone projection from a wall to give support and strength.

cap house A small tower on top of a larger tower or keep above the roof stairway.

caryatid A sculpted figure (usually female) serving as a column or pillar.

corbel A small projection, or series of projections, one above the other, cantilevered out from a wall to take a superimposed load, or sometimes affecting to.

Corinthian pillar Type of Roman pillar or column with an ornate capital of carved acanthus leaves.

crenelled Battlemented, divided into crenelles (spaces) and merlons (stonework).

crowstep Steps down either side of a gable, often quoins.

curtain The wall surrounding a bailey.

donjon A type of keep, often round.

dormer window Window with a gable, projecting from a sloping roof.

enciente An outer curtain wall.

entresol Low storey between the first and the ground floor; a mezzanine floor.

fanlight An arched window above a door.

finial The decorated terminal on the apex of a gable; the top part of a pinnacle.

fortalice The outline of a fortification; small fort.

fosse A ditch or moat.

freestone Any stone that cuts well in all directions, especially fine-grained sandstone or limestone.

frieze A decorated band along the upper part of an internal wall.

gable The triangular part of an exterior wall between the top of the side-walls and the slopes on the roof, or a similar structure above a window or door.

garderobe Latrine.

gatehouse Part of a castle including the main gate which eventually replaced the keep.

gazebo A lookout tower on the roof, sometimes called a belvedere.

Gothic Of the Middle Ages.

Jacobean Architecture in Britain dating from 1603 to 1625.

joists Beams that hold up a floor.

keep The great tower or strongest part of a castle.

loggia A gallery open on one side, sometimes pillared.

loops Holes or slits through which arrows and guns were fired.

machicolations Stone platforms built out from battlements, with holes in the floor for dropping missiles, pouring boiling oil, etc, found mainly over gateways.

minstrel's gallery A type of indoor balcony or loggia for containing singers and musicians.

mouldings Carvings in the undercurve of an arch or on a cornice, etc.

Neo-Classical Architecture of the late 18th century based on Classical principles.

Neo-Tudor Architectural design based on the Tudor period of 1485–1558.

newel The upright column around which the steps of a circular staircase wind.

ogee arch An arch having a double curved line either side of the central point with a convex and a concave part.

ogee roof A roof in the shape of an ogee arch.

oratory A small private chapel in a castle or great house.

oriel A type of upper-floor bay window on corbelling.

Palladian In the style of the 16th-century Italian architect Andrea Palladio.

parapet The part of a wall that rises above roof level at the top of a building.

pediment Classical equivalent of the gable, usually triangular but likely to be curved or arched in Baroque architecture. Smaller versions appear above doors and windows of Neo-Classical and Baroque and similar styles.

pend Scots word for a vaulted archway.

piscina A stone basin (usually in a church) for washing vessels.

portcullis An iron or wooden grilled gate made to slide up and down in vertical grooves in the doorposts of a castle entrance.

quoins Corner stones around a door or window, often of dressed stone.

range A wing or block of a castle or palace.

Renaissance 15th- and 16th-century style based on Classical principles.

Rococo Not a style in its own right but the last phase of Baroque, generally more flamboyant.

Romanesque The style current until the advent of Gothic. Though incorporated into Anglo-Saxon architecture, this style is usually associated with the Norman.

rounds Expanding, rounded open angles on a parapet.

rubble facade Course or rough stone used for the facade of a building. There are several different types including rough, coursed and square.

staggered corbelling Corbelling in two alternating steps.

tracery Ornamental intersecting work in a window, screen or panel, also used decoratively within arches and vaults.

turnpike A stone spiral staircase, usually in an extended tower.

vault An arched ceiling or roof. A barrel vault resembles the roof of a tunnel, a groined vault the roof of two intersecting tunnels and a rib vault the roofs of two intersecting Gothic arched tunnels.

wheel stair A type of spiral stair.